MAPPING YOUR LEGACY

The Peregrinzilla Press

ATLANTA

MAPPING YOUR YOUR LEGACY

A Hook-It-Up Journey

Charlie Eitel

For all my associates at
Interface, Inc.
worldwide.

ACKNOWLEDGMENTS

I WOULD LIKE TO THANK my executive assistant, Linda Timms, and our receptionist/administrative assistant, Cindy Stringer, for their tireless hours of typing and continuously adjusting this text to get it "just right."

I would also like to acknowledge my daughter, Jennifer Eitel Young, for her thorough review and recommendations. She got a chance to employ her degree in English.

I also want to thank the following people for their support, recommendations, and editing: Marsha Kerestes, Ray Willoch, J. Zink and Jeffrey Zink.

Charlie Eitel
Atlanta, Georgia, 1998

IN 1995, I published my first book, *Eitel Time: Turnaround Secrets*. Prior to the first printing, I asked several close friends to give me their opinion of the text. Almost without exception, everyone said more, indicating that my work was incomplete, or maybe suggesting that I needed to use more examples to make my points. As you might expect, I accepted all the feedback I could get and used many of the suggested corrections and additions. Down deep in my heart, I knew the book needed more, but I was tired and wanted to bring the project to an end. Both my wife, Cindy, and my executive assistant, Linda Timms, agreed that they did not have the energy to read the text *one more time,* so I declared the book finished.

Eitel Time: Turnaround Secrets changed my life because of the hundreds of letters I received from people all over the world, telling me how the book affected their lives, and caused them to stop and more closely examine their priorities. In *Eitel Time* I tried to explore the question of why we do what we do with our lives. It was sort of an attempt to get people to look in the mirror, and ask themselves if they were really living a life of true happiness. The book you are about to read expands on my original thinking and stories, but is more of a roadmap. I guess you could say it is more instructional and therefore is more about *how* than *why.*

I have read more books in the last three years than in the previous 15 years of my life, in search of the knowledge, creativity and confidence to put on paper what I believe are solid points about how to logically share my experiences and ideas in a format that is easy to understand and apply.

Hopefully, *Mapping Your Legacy* will give you the simple tools you need to create your vision and never look back.

CONTENTS

I LOVE TO READ – *how about you? I have no way of knowing why you have* Mapping Your Legacy *in your hands, but I sincerely hope you will read it in its entirety.*

My friends and associates know that I love to read. I guess that's why I continuously receive all sorts of books and articles from them. For some reason, I have a hard time starting thick books, and unless the first few pages really grab me, *I am likely to go on to the next read. My guess is that you and I have this in common. I also find that most books are written by people from academia, who are seldom able to use their* own stories and experiences *as the center of the text, but rather they write about what others have done.* Mapping Your Legacy *is not about me, but it was written solely by me based on 48 years of my life's learning experiences.*

I have had the honor to be president of four companies since graduating from college in 1971. Even though my career has been predominantly focused on the floorcoverings industry, I have always viewed myself as being in the people business. As you read Mapping Your Legacy, *you will glean that my mission is to be sure that I support the hearts and souls of the people with whom I work.*

I have written all 12 chapters as if I were talking to you. Even though we may not know each other, I sincerely hope you will feel like we are having a conversation that you can relate to and enjoy; so if you're ready, let's get started.

CREATING A VISION

I

The power and creativity of the human mind is underutilized in this world, so why not liberate it?

IN ORDER to create a viable vision you must answer one very fundamental question, "What do I really want?" If you don't know, you should start allowing time to dream, and if you do know, I suggest that you start setting priorities. If you are not sure, you may want to do both.

Let's talk about dreaming and setting priorities. One of my favorite sayings is, "What the mind can conceive and believe, it can achieve."[1] If you can see an event, a potential accomplishment or anything that you want to be a part of your future, then you can dream with vision. What keeps us from dreaming? All of us want to fantasize about the things that we want and do not have, and then we often hear a little voice inside us that whispers, "Nice try, now come back to reality." One of the unique traits of visionaries is that they have the ability to stand in the present and describe the future, often in great detail, because they do not see the obstacles that others do. "Obstacles are those

---
[1] Napoleon Hill

frightful things we see when we take our eyes off our goals."[2] It is very easy for all of us to come up with reasons why we are not entitled to dream and create our own vision. If you are thinking that way, it is because you, alone, established such rules.

For the last 16 years, I have had the honor and pleasure of working with a very special lady, Linda Timms, my executive assistant. A few years ago, she cross-stitched and framed a quote for me, which I think about daily. It reads, "Faith sees the invisible, believes the incredible, and receives the impossible."[3] "What we need is more people who specialize in the impossible."[4]

In order to see your vision, you must be able to believe what you see. I have found one of the best ways to convince yourself that your vision is achievable is to write it down in your own handwriting. (I don't mean type it on your computer.) Writing words in your handwriting creates a more permanent, believable, mental image. Your individual handwriting is special because there is no one else in the world who has handwriting just like yours. Seeing your dreams on paper forms a clearer vision of your desires, and makes your goals seem more possible. This is why I have taken the liberty of altering the famous saying I quoted earlier to read, "What the mind can conceive, believe and *write down*, it can achieve."

Why don't people want to write down their dreams and goals? Maybe because they are afraid someone might see

2 Hannah Moore
3 Unknown
4 Theodore Roethke

what they have committed to writing, and challenge and/or judge them if their dreams or goals don't come true. Let's identify the problem as *fear of failure* because that is exactly what we are talking about — fear. Can you imagine what you would try if you knew you could not fail?

When I think of the words, *fear* and *failure*, I am reminded of the life of Abraham Lincoln. Despite the many crises he faced in his life, he became the President of the United States at the age of 51, even after a series of disappointments that will strike you as unbelievable when you read about them.

Age

22 FAILED IN BUSINESS

23 RAN FOR THE LEGISLATURE AND WAS DEFEATED

24 AGAIN FAILED IN BUSINESS

25 ELECTED TO THE LEGISLATURE

26 SWEETHEART DIED

27 HAD A NERVOUS BREAKDOWN

29 DEFEATED FOR SPEAKER

31 DEFEATED FOR ELECTOR

34 DEFEATED FOR CONGRESS

37 ELECTED TO CONGRESS

39 DEFEATED FOR CONGRESS

46 DEFEATED FOR THE SENATE

47 DEFEATED FOR VICE PRESIDENT

49 DEFEATED FOR THE SENATE

51 ELECTED PRESIDENT OF THE UNITED STATES

When I am dreaming and creating a specific vision, I try to remove my fears from the past and imagined barriers and force myself to do four things.

1. I WRITE DOWN MY SPECIFIC VISION AND/OR DREAMS AND GOALS.
2. I GO THROUGH A MENTAL EXERCISE WHEREBY I CONVINCE MYSELF THAT WHAT I SEE IS POSSIBLE.
3. I ARTICULATE A PROCESS TO ACHIEVE THE VISION, A *STORY*, IF YOU WILL, THAT I CAN BELIEVE AND VISUALIZE BEING IMPLEMENTED.
4. I TELL SEVERAL PEOPLE, WHOM I KNOW AND RESPECT, EXACTLY WHAT MY VISION IS AND WHAT IT WILL LOOK LIKE WHEN I GET THERE.

By going through this methodology, I involve and often enroll others in formalizing my vision and, as a result, simultaneously commit myself to make my vision a reality.

When you tell people whom you respect what your specific vision is, you signal your intention. Intention is a powerful force that comes from the Latin word which means "to stretch." Intention also gives you a visionary context in which your specific thoughts are organized. Intention is how you want the game to come out in context and process.

In the last few years, I have had the pleasure of getting to know Bill McDonough, who owns an architectural firm in Charlottesville, Virginia. He is also the Dean of Architecture at the University of Virginia. In a presentation Bill gave to our employees last year at our world meeting, he asked, "Who was the captain of the Titanic when it sank?" No one seemed to have the answer. I suspect everyone was trying to think of a specific person's name. They realized that they were on the wrong track when they heard Bill answer his own question, "The designer was the captain of the ship." If you have seen the movie, you will really be able to relate to his point: there were only half as many life boats as were needed to evacuate the ship when fully occupied. According to Bill, design is a manifestation of human intention. The designer of the Titanic failed to be fully accountable for his vision, which resulted in a disaster that no one would intentionally plan. So use your dreams to design and visualize your intention. You can then become both the designer and captain of your own ship.

One of the ways to be sure that your intentions are good is to focus your thoughts on how to help other people. Good things are a lot more likely to happen to you if your thoughts are focused on how you would use your good fortune to help others. After all, you get what you give. Making money is a by-product of doing the right thing and helping others get what they want.

My friend, Ken Kragen, is a great example of someone who believes in giving. You may recall that Ken was the creator and organizer of the "We Are The World" African relief effort. In his book, *Life is a Contact Sport,* Ken reveals the challenges he faced in making this historical event happen. Ken also was the creator of the fund raising event, "Hands Across America." Combined, these two initiatives raised over $101 million for programs to help society's disadvantaged.

Ken is the best event planner I have ever known because his vision enables him to blow right through any obstacles that are in his path. He is a visionary, a dreamer, and a person who delivers results. Ken never seems to worry about what he gets, only what he gives, and at the same time has done quite well financially.

There are two words that you need to take out of your vocabulary when you are dreaming: *is* and *because.* When you take the *is* out, you open up the possibilities for change. When you take the *because* out, you let go of the belief that you know the reason something happened.

Change can be a powerful force but it is also one with which many people have great difficulty. Last year my wife, Cindy, decided to go back to college to finish course work toward her bachelor's degree after a 27 year break. She could have convinced herself that going back to college *is too difficult*; or she could have listened to self-talk that might have said, "I am afraid I won't make good grades *because* it has been so many years since I was in school." With total support from her friends and all of our family, she let go of *is* and *because* and has a 3.6 grade point average on a scale of 4.0 after her first year as a full-time student. All my encouragement cost me was having to adjust to eating TV dinners three nights a week, but it has been well worth it to see her so excited about learning.

If you are having trouble taking a risk like Cindy did, and if you are having trouble dreaming, here is a tip. Think about all the things that are important to you in life and blend those thoughts with what you are doing when you are the happiest. Then push yourself outside your comfort zone into your dreaming zone to create a vision and an intention of what you want. More specifically, envision what makes you happy and visually place yourself in that environment. Once you see yourself in the future, you will then be able to set the proper priorities in order to thrust yourself to your envisioned landing place.

The more often you dream and the more often your dreams become reality, you will realize that there is not enough time in life to manifest all the things you want to do. The key here is to clearly figure out what you are enthusiastic about and then become great at it. Don't worry about running out of time, but get started.

One of my heroes, the late George Burns said, "If I had known I was going to live this long, I would have taken better care of myself." George passed away in 1996 at the age of 100. I suggest you take care of yourself, and plan to live to be over 100 years old, so you will have the time to more fully realize as many of life's opportunities as possible.

You may note that I am now talking more about dreams than vision. The word *dream* may be easier to grasp since it is something we all do, versus the word *vision*, which can be somewhat intimidating. In order to try to overcome the fear of committing yourself to your dreams, it is essential that you have a strong connection to your story. It is important that you be able to express and understand your full and undivided self. Work hard to understand your past programming and use your experiences and intuition as a source of strength and learning.

Sometimes it is easy to convince yourself that certain people whom you admire have a perfect life. It is therefore very common to make up beliefs such as "John, Bill, or Linda have it all." The reality is, no one *has it all.* Everyone has problems and a past which result in varying degrees of pain. Learn to use your story and experiences as sources of power through storytelling and even confession. What you are looking for is a combination of logic and intuition.

Creating a vision can be a spiritual experience, and there is clearly a place for spirituality in the workplace. I am not talking about religious beliefs since religion is an organized form of spirituality, but rather to seek the common threads of what your working environment can look like in an ideal situation. Specifically, I'm talking about creating an environment where people look forward to getting up and going to work.

Years ago, one of my visions was to create a corporate

culture for associates where everyone could experience shared values that are interchangeable at work and at home. After all, most of us spend most of our waking hours at work to earn a living, so we can provide for our families, and in fact, be at home with them.

In 1997 and 1998, Ann Goodman and Charles Fishman, freelance writers representing *Fast Company* magazine, spent countless hours learning and writing about our company. In April 1998, *Fast Company* published a wonderful article, of which all of us at Interface are very proud. After Charles interviewed me, he shared a story about a conversation he had with one of our employees he met during his tour of our facilities. Barbara Smith, who works in the tufting department at our Ray C. Anderson plant in West Point, Georgia, said, "Interface is such an important part of my life, I would come to work everyday, even if I didn't get paid." This story may seem incredible but, given her sincerity, it appears to validate that her job is more important to her than money.

Our company was highlighted again in 1998 by *Fortune* magazine as one of the top 100 companies to work for in America. This recognition was based on an internal survey conducted with a random cross-section of our employees. I must say that this specific recognition is the highest form of flattery, and I believe further confirms that we do, in fact, have the kind of company that people want to get up in the morning and go to work for.

I am amazed by the wide gap of behavior that exists in the world between the people who love their work and those who do not. This gap is often a result of people believing that they do not have the power to make a difference and that their views will not be recognized and acted on. The reality is that the best organizations in the world want their employees to think independently and feel empowered. Over the years, I have observed with interest companies who routinely employ industrial engineers to conduct *time and motion* studies on how employees perform their duties. It seems to me that companies should rather focus on what is more important, which are people's *minds and notions*.

When I joined Interface in 1993, one of the first things my leadership team did was to help create a vision of the future for all associates. Through a *SWOT* (strengths, weaknesses, opportunities and threats) exercise, we collectively envisioned our future and committed to writing specific plans mapping the creation of a company which, if it existed two years later, would put us out of business. We wrote lengthy paragraphs in the present tense, describing what our customers, employees, community and suppliers would say about us in two years. Then our team set our goals toward becoming that company. We created a vision and then pulled toward it.

Before the two year time period passed, we became too comfortable with our vision, and have since recreated another, more powerful and accountable version, which you will learn more about in the coming pages. A periodic updating of your vision will keep you sharp, growing and competitive.

Remember, what the mind can conceive, believe and write down, it can achieve.

The power and creativity of the human mind is underutilized in this world, so why not liberate it? The first step toward this liberation belongs to you. It is your responsibility to your own soul.

KEEPING IT SIMPLE

II

I have always believed that the leader of an organization should be able to describe what his or her company stands for and is trying to become in less than 15 minutes.

HENRY DAVID THOREAU said that the three things we all need to do to be happy are to *simplify, simplify, simplify.*

A couple of summers ago, we took a family vacation to Europe and spent the majority of our time in France, which included four days in Paris. We had the opportunity to spend the better part of a day in the Louvre, which many people believe contains the most magnificent collection of art in the world. If you've been there, you know that a one day visit does not do it justice, and in fact, I doubt a week would. As we worked our way through this massive structure and seemingly endless displays of art, I began to notice signs directing visitors to the *Mona Lisa*. After we viewed the magnificent sculptures, frescoes and every other form of art imaginable, with all their complexity, uniqueness and beauty, we finally found the *Mona Lisa*.

As I stood looking at this relatively small painting of a woman with a simple smile on her face, it occurred to me how incredible it is that this hugely famous painting is, in fact, so simple.

When I joined Interface Flooring Systems as President and Chief Executive Officer in November 1993, I soon discovered that I had inherited a division of the company that had become so complex that virtually no one understood what to do next.

My new leadership team spent the first few months trying to mentally reverse-engineer the thinking that had led to such complexity. Within about two months, it became clear that there were three fundamental problems: 1) We had evolved into a pattern of following our competitors' styling (of product) instead of being the leader. 2) We were attempting to run a business with the belief that we could routinely predict what the customer wanted to buy. 3) We were manufacturing the majority of our products on a *make to inventory* basis versus *make to order*.

One of the first decisions I made was to make it clear to our employees that we would never again attempt to duplicate any of our competitors' products. The second major change we implemented was to shift to a *systems approach to manufacturing,* which caused us to coin the phrase, "simple input, pretty output." I later learned a new word, "dymaxion," which means, "Getting the maximum output from minimum energy." Believing that it is impossible to accurately predict what today's discriminating buyer wants, we created a simplified core of feeder raw materials that enabled us to rapidly bring a vast array of standard products to market, and simultaneously create and deliver custom options quicker than any of our competitors. For example, when I arrived on the scene we were producing one carpet tile product that required over 100 different colors of yarn from what we call "the input side of design," and it resulted in less than 50 finished colors. Today, those numbers are dramatically reversed, whereby we use approximately 50 different yarn colors and produce over 1,000 standard finished colors, plus custom options. We no longer need to worry about predicting our customers' future preferences. We have rather created the future by developing a system which enables us to respond to our customers' exact needs.

I have always believed that the leader of an organization should be able to describe what his or her company stands for and is trying to become in less than 15 minutes, a feat pretty hard to do in this fast paced, complicated world we live in today. Within a few months after my arrival at Interface, I began to visualize and create what has now become known as the *Interface wheel*. In *Eitel Time: Turnaround Secrets* I briefly discussed how this model evolved, but as I indicated in the preface, I failed to fully explain the history of how my vision evolved to the forming of this model. This is an easy map to comprehend

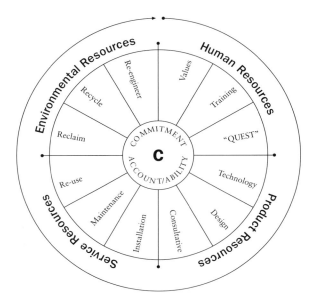

that I believe all Interface associates in our floorcovering businesses understand today.

The wheel is representative of how any organizational model can work in today's environment versus the traditional and hierarchical military model that most of us learned in school. Military models can be very effective in war time because you are likely to be in a crisis situation where people can get killed. Such models simply do not work in today's business world, and why should they? We are supposed to be at peace — not war.

In referencing my model, you will notice the *C* in the center of the wheel, which stands for our customers. I often further refer to my wheel as our accountability circle, pointing out that we are, in fact, accountable to our customers whom we place in the center of our universe. As you can observe from the model, we provide *Human Resources, Product Resources, Service Resources* and *Environmental Resources*. This enables our customers to draw on any of our competencies (call it benchmarking if you like).

The model is also intended to be multidimensional and representative of a closed loop system, much like nature's efficient, closed loop processes. Another way to describe this point is, "We all report to our customers."

In nature, there is no such thing as waste because one species' waste is another's food. My friend, Bill McDonough, was one of the first to coin the phrase, "Waste = Food." In the living organization, all resources are available to other resources, and particularly to the customer, who, after all, is the lifeblood which enables the company to exist in the first place.

No organization can survive over an extended period of time without the proper focus on people as its most important resource. The key is to understand the importance of treating associates with respect and dignity, and ultimately living the Golden Rule: "Do unto others as you would have them do unto you." That is why I began my model identifying the importance of human resources. From there, it's much easier to determine the needed technology, design, sales, and services to follow. In our case, services include turnkey installation, maintenance, reusing, and eventually the reclaiming, recycling and re-engineering of our products at the highest possible natural level in the food chain.

As I developed this model, I tested it on many of our associates. Once they understood it and gave me their feedback and support, I used the model to communicate the future vision of our company. Within less than a year, almost every associate worldwide understood our vision, and today they can communicate it themselves in a logical manner in less than 15 minutes. We are now in the process of modifying this model to represent all of Interface rather than just the floorcoverings segment.

Most people learn more quickly when they have a *graphic* that they can image. That is why I think everyone in a leadership position should figure out how to create their own simplified, graphic model, reflecting their specific vision. One way to try out this idea is to stop right now and write down (in order of priority) what your organization is trying to become. You can start by using my wheel format if you like. Take my words out and give it a try. You can do this for your personal life as well. When I was developing this model, I realized that it not only replicated the closed loop system in nature, but also how one's life may be lived as well. This thought is actually what inspired me to write *Eitel Time: Turnaround Secrets*. When I was trying to create an outline for the book, I began by asking myself, "What do I want most out of my life?" My answer was, and still is today, three words, "Peace of Mind," so that became the final chapter. I then began to think logically of the things I believed I needed to do to achieve peace of mind, which resulted in the titles of the chapters in the following order:

1. MAKING A DIFFERENCE
2. DOING WHAT'S RIGHT
3. TRUSTING INTENTIONS
4. PLAYING TO WIN
5. WALKING YOUR TALK
6. BUILDING YOUR TEAM
7. HELPING OTHERS
8. TAKING CARE OF YOURSELF
9. HAVING FUN
10. BEING ACCOUNTABLE
11 REFLECTING TIME
12. PEACE OF MIND

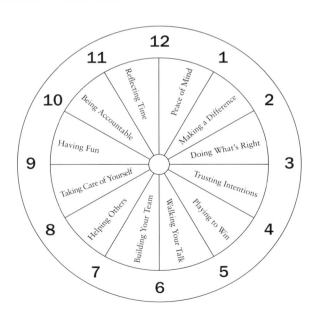

EITEL TIME: TURNAROUND SECRETS

If you don't stand for something, you might fall for anything, so you may as well get busy and start setting your own priorities, thus creating your vision in a systematic fashion that reflects who you are and what you want to be. This approach to simplification, while a challenge, will bring you confidence, comfort and a sense of inner peace that will enable you to explain to your associates and family your vision and what it will look like when you get there. Most people spend more time planning their vacations than they do their lives. You can be different.

SETTING PRIORITIES

III

People want freedom of choice but are confused by the huge choices they have.

WE LIVE IN a complex world full of mixed messages and unpredictable behavior of today's consumer. In recent years, I have become quite amazed with the wide range of differences in what people say they want and what they actually do. As Andrew Carnegie said, "As I grow older, I pay less attention to what people say — I just watch what they do."

People seem to want safety but nevertheless yearn for excitement and danger. Maybe this explains why bungee jumping is the fastest growing fad in the world, and plenty dangerous.

People usually say they want something new, but choose the classic. For example, in our business, we find that earth tone colors always dominate our sales, regardless of color trends.

People want freedom of choice but are confused by the huge choices they have. How many times have you felt the stress of trying to order dinner from a complex menu, knowing that you purposely went to the restaurant in the first place because of the wide range of quality choices available?

People want more information but yearn for silence and tranquillity. Maybe this is why massage therapy is the fastest growing profession in the world. We are all trying to find a way to relax our minds and bodies from the information overload to which we are exposed.

These notions and beliefs caused me to focus on some serious concerns I have about the world we live in today, and at the same time, share a few stories about my own good and bad choices that may be helpful to you as you set priorities and simplify your life.

CONCERN:

We spend too much time and effort today trying to accumulate material possessions (our wants).

STORY:

We all dream of having material possessions, and I am no different. When Cindy and I were first married, I had a vision that one day we would be able to afford a ski condominium in Colorado. I have never viewed myself as money-motivated, but I did have a clear vision of owning a second home. Subconsciously, I believe I thought owning a vacation home where we could take the kids (we hoped to have) fit in with one of my core values — which is to spend as much time as possible with my family.

By the time I was 36 years old, we had a three-bedroom, three-bath condo in Steamboat Springs, Colorado, worth as much as our home. We enjoyed the condo, but after about three years, I realized that the worry of a second home made me more unhappy than happy, and eventually, we sold it.

Today, we enjoy the same privileges by simply renting and are no longer burdened with the responsibility and financial pressure. We use our energy instead to receive what is more important in life — getting our emotional needs met, which include love, affection, peace, happiness and spirituality.

CONCERN:

Our daily lives move at a record pace and families are losing their connectivity.

STORY:

When Cindy and I began having children, we made a conscious decision to settle for less so she could focus her attention on raising our kids.

I clearly recognize that many couples want dual careers. This is a choice I certainly support if that's what they need, as long as they are not confusing needs and wants. I also recognize that some parents have no choice except to work.

I believe there are two main problems that cause people to feel forced to work against their true wishes: 1) the excessive income tax structure that exists in the western world; and 2) a feeling that they must *keep up with the Jones's,* which is magnified by heavy advertising, loose credit policies of the financial service companies, and the many vendors selling what seems like an endless array of merchandise.

The Eitel kids have turned out great, and I believe it is because Cindy was there for them during their formative years. She did her first and foremost job perfectly, which was raising our children. As I said before, she is now back in school and will soon complete her degree in Interior Design, and is getting both her needs and wants met.

CONCERN:

We are in the *information age* and gaining new knowledge at an unprecedented rate, which often violates people's privacy and much needed quiet time.

STORY:

Over the years, I have been kidded about taking time off. I am known for my four to five day getaways and regular family vacations, which are usually focused on some sort of sports activity. Like most of us, I am chained to voice mail, and in recent months, e-mail. I love information just like you do, but I am convinced that I can do just fine with a break from real time information every once in a while. The main reason that I have comfort with this belief is because I work with such great people who know their jobs and are not afraid to make decisions without me. They get the information I miss when I am off recharging my battery, and when I return, I often realize that half of what I missed, I didn't need to know immediately anyway. I find it quite amusing to receive written and electronic correspondence, and realize that by the time I can respond to the question, someone else, who was closer to the issue, already has done so. Learn not to let information overload bog you down. Stop and smell the roses along the way.

CONCERN:

It is hard to find role models and leaders.

STORY:

In Chapter One, I spoke of the importance of having a strong connection to your own story. A big part of everyone's story has a lot to do with "mom and dad."

Our parents are our first role models in life, and I have been very fortunate to have two wonderful parents. My mother died when I was nine years old, but I am certain that she had a lot to do with the happiness I have been blessed with in my life. After my mother's death, my dad and I became very close, because he was able to fill the void created by my mother's death until I could accept this difficult reality.

The problem we often have as children is coming to grips with the fact that our parents are a product of their parents, and that they experienced a completely different childhood than we did. This point is magnified by the fact that their parents had different parents and so on. My friend, Dr. J. Zink, gave me some good advice a couple of years ago when I was having trouble communicating with my son, Chuck. He said, "Just pretend you're his uncle and watch what happens." As usual, J. was exactly right. Chuck and I have a great relationship today.

I believe the best way to be a role model is to quit judging others and do the best you can to set the right examples through your own actions. No one is perfect, yet we can all strive for and model excellence. The following comparison between excellence and perfection was placed on my desk one day by someone who never identified themselves, but I think it says it all.

Perfection is being right,
Excellence is willing to be wrong.
Perfection is fear,
Excellence is taking a risk.
Perfection is anger and frustration,
Excellence is powerful.
Perfection is control,
Excellence is spontaneous.
Perfection is judgment,
Excellence is accepting.
Perfection is taking,
Excellence is giving.
Perfection is doubt,
Excellence is confidence.
Perfection is pressure,
Excellence is natural.
Perfection is the destination,
Excellence is the journey.

We all need to be role models of excellence rather than perfection.

CONCERN:

Our western civilization has become very wasteful.

STORY:

Nature can meet our needs, but it will not survive our greed unless we quickly change.

Interface's Chairman, Ray Anderson, recently published a wonderful book entitled, *Mid-Course Correction,* which clearly explains the magnitude of the waste that exists in the world. There is no way I can cover in one or two paragraphs the essence of his book, but I respectfully ask that you read it, and then you will get a comprehensive view on this subject and his efforts to change the tide. This subject is also covered in considerable detail in Chapter Nine, "Understanding Sustainability."

A little over 100 years ago, there was no such thing as left and right shoes, and today, we have left and right snow skis. Seventy-five years ago, Henry Ford said, "I don't care what color of car we manufacture, as long as it's black." Today, there are virtually limitless options in automobiles. We live in a world of many choices, which on the one hand is great, and on the other, can be quite stressful unless we set priorities that facilitate enjoyment and affordability.

I hope this chapter has helped you focus on the importance of setting priorities. Hopefully, you are now more able to create your own uncomplicated vision for the future, thereby bringing you a greater sense of calmness and peace of mind.

SELECTING PEOPLE

IV

*As a leader of our company,
my job is to find and recruit leaders.*

ON MORE than one occasion, I have been asked to identify what I believe to be the most important part of my job. For me, the answer is easy — picking the right people to lead our company and being sure that their core competencies are optimized for everyone's benefit, including their own. More simply stated, as a leader of our company, my job is to find and recruit leaders.

Over the years, I have resolved that leaders have five characteristics that I want to share with you. My starting point is to accept the fact that I am only as good as my leadership team, because I certainly do not have the complete range of knowledge and experience to be an expert on all disciplines of business.

Two of my favorite quotes referencing the importance of selecting people are as follows:

"There is something that is much more scarce, something much rarer than ability. It is the ability to recognize ability."[5]

5 Robert Half

"When you hire people smarter than you are, you prove that you are smarter than they are."[6]

CHARACTERISTIC #1: HIRE PEOPLE WHO DO NOT HAVE TO BE MANAGED.

These are people who are committed to doing a good job, even when they don't feel like it, because they have grown up in an environment where somehow they learned to be reliable. They have a natural sense of conscience and dedication to their mission, and create a sense of purpose in their work.

CHARACTERISTIC #2: HIRE PEOPLE WHO ARE ACCOUNTABLE.

We all report to the outcome of the results that we are trying to produce. People who are accountable make commitments and deliver results on time and often ahead of schedule. They don't blame other people or events beyond their control for the difficulties they encounter, but rather figure out how to cross the finish line on time. They figure out how to engage others to help them achieve their goals, and also share the rewards once the mission is accomplished.

My late grandmother, Clyde Cordellia Crumbley (wow, what a name!), used to routinely say, "Will you, won't you, can you, can't you, aren't you gonna? Please do. I declare, you said you would, now won't you?" As you can tell from her slang, she was from the South. She got quite irritated at people who did not keep their commitments. Her peculiar Southern saying has stuck with me over the years and has

---

[6] R.H. Grant

continually reminded me of the importance of being accountable.

CHARACTERISTIC #3: HIRE PEOPLE WHO ARE DRIVEN.

People who are driven set lofty goals and usually commit themselves beyond their natural ability. They have a bias for action, but they also understand the importance of producing quality work. They understand the importance of speed and realize they determine the pace of the team. People who are driven realize they are going to make mistakes, but they believe they have a responsibility to take risks in order to continually find new and better ways to do things.

"One person's belief is equal to a force of 49 who only have interest."[7] People who are driven inherently know that they must push themselves to places they have never been before to test limits and break through barriers.

CHARACTERISTIC #4: HIRE PEOPLE WHO ARE ETHICAL.

People who are ethical automatically assume that everything they do or say is likely to be public knowledge. This is not to say they have an aversion for the spotlight. They simply believe that their work is a self-portrait. They continually judge themselves rather than others and pride themselves in knowing the difference between right and wrong.

They are loaded with character and can clearly distinguish the colors black, white and gray.

"Character is the ability to say no, when everyone

7 John Stuart Mill

except your conscience is screaming yes."[8] When ethical people do make mistakes (ultimately everyone does), they immediately correct the error and take full responsibility.

CHARACTERISTIC #5: HIRE PEOPLE WHO ARE VISIONARY.

In Chapter One, I discussed the power of creating a vision, and yet, you will notice I have listed the criterion of being a visionary as number five in importance on my list of how I pick people. Here's why! We know the awesome cost of vision without integrity. Vision is only a virtue after you recognize the importance of being accountable and ethical.

Visionaries often do not want to conform to the status quo but rather insist on finding a better way.

For the last ten years, I have had the pleasure of working closely with David Oakey, the owner of David Oakey Designs, located in LaGrange, Georgia. David is head of product design for Interface's global floorcoverings group. He and I share a core value and that is, "Never knock off a competitor's product." If you follow the floorcoverings industry, you know that Interface has not been shy in making sure our competitors extend us the same courtesy. David is a true visionary when it comes to figuring out how to continually re-engineer the products we sell. I recently saw a poem which reminded me of his visionary talent and values, which I want to share with you. "They copied all they could follow but they couldn't copy my mind, and I left 'em all sweatin' and stealin' — a year and a half behind."[9]

---

[8] Richie Harris
[9] Rudyard Kipling

As I stated earlier, I joined Interface in 1993, with my original assignment being to help re-engineer and turn around Interface Flooring Systems, located in LaGrange, Georgia. This business was the original company founded by our Chairman, Ray Anderson, in 1973. By 1993, Interface, Inc. had become quite large, and the people responsible for this division had, in my view, lost their way. In less than one year, our team got this business back on track, and Ray decided I should play a bigger role, so I was given the assignment to run our worldwide floorcoverings operations. In conjunction with this new responsibility, Ray and I decided to take our top team on a four-day team building retreat in hopes of gaining consensus support for the new direction in which we wanted to take the company. We selected Larry Wilson's Pecos River ranch, located in Santa Fe, New Mexico, as the site and retained Pecos River Learning Center to facilitate our meeting. (We have since formed our own learning company, called "*one world learning*," that you will hear more about later.) The Interface management group that I inherited was somewhat disjointed, and I can assure you that we were far from being a team.

During my opening comments, shortly after our arrival at the ranch, I stated to our group of 14 that our objective was to create a high-performing team. I further stated that as far as I was concerned, the past was history, and suggested that we all start anew by clearing out *our old maps,* and focus on the future.

I made it clear that the only way Interface ultimately would be successful was for us to model team behavior for the rest of our associates. I asked our group to work hard during the upcoming four days to become a championship team instead of a team of champions. As it turned out, we weren't even a team of champions — over half the group never made the transition to the new company that was emerging.

It took three years to recreate and jell our top team (the Peregrinzillas), but we finally did it in January of 1998. During the transition we never really fired any of the original Peregrinzillas, but rather allowed them to make their own choices, through their actions, as to whether or not they wanted to be on our team. You may be wondering, what the heck is a Peregrinzilla? As part of our experiential learning activities, we ask all of our teams to come up with a name of an animal to describe their team. A Peregrinzilla is a cross between a peregrine falcon (the world's fastest flying bird) and Godzilla. I know this sounds crazy, but stay with me.

Today, we are a championship team that I will put up against the best of the best. We are all friends and share a level of mutual respect that is clearly helping our company reach new heights we only dreamed of four years ago. In January of 1998 our team wrote a purpose statement as follows:

THE PEREGRINZILLAS' PURPOSE: THE PEREGRINZILLAS
IS A LEADERSHIP TEAM SERVING THE WHOLE OF INTERFACE,
INC. OUR PURPOSE IS TO VISUALIZE AND FACILITATE A
FUTURE IN WHICH INTERFACE IS: SUSTAINABLE, A LEARNING
CULTURE AND GLOBALLY CONNECTED FOR THE BENEFIT OF
OUR PEOPLE, PLACE AND PRODUCT; OUR CUSTOMERS AND
OTHER STAKEHOLDERS.

Sometimes we get to hand-pick the people we work
with and sometimes we inherit them. Either way, the
leader's job is to create an environment that enables people
to make choices about what is right for them. Along these
lines, I strive to enforce only one rule, which is, "We will be
a team." And today, with the current players, we are.

Selecting people is the most important part of my job;
however, people also have to be developed through
mentoring and continuous education. At Interface, ongoing
education is a way of life. Over the last five years, we have
put our money where our mouth is. Any associate of our
company can finish his or her high school education (GED)
at company expense, and in some cases, even on company
time. If the associate wants to go to college, we will pay
those expenses as well, provided the associate makes a
sincere effort to perform.

A few years ago, I was asked a question by a reporter
from *The Wall Street Journal* about the costs associated
with our educational programs. The reporter asked, "How

do you know when you get your money back from your educational programs?" I answered, "We don't." He further asked, "What about those people who quit? Isn't that expensive for the company?" I said, "Look, my job is to create an environment where people want to work, not to worry about the choice they may make to leave." Today at Interface, our employee turnover is so low that we don't even routinely measure it.

I will close this chapter with a quote from my friend, Richie Harris, with Sales Recruiters International, Ltd., which I think sums up what selecting people is all about. "Anybody can get a position that they can grow out of. I help people attain positions that they can grow into."

BEING A ROLE MODEL

V

*I believe there is one very important trait
that almost all people recognize in others,
and that is sincerity.*

WE ARE ALL the sum total of the influence of our role models,
education and experiences. Most of us end up with three
categories of mentors or role models who guide our lives:
1) Mom and Dad; 2) people other than our parents who
show a sincere interest in us; and 3) people we have
little or no relationship with, but whom we admire for
their accomplishments, status and perceived power (e.g.,
professional athletes).

For most of us, our first role models are Mom and Dad.
If you are a parent, you know that by the time you figure
out how to be a parent, your kids are grown! After all, we
are not taught how to be a parent in high school or college.
If you want some help along this line, I recommend that
you read a book by my close friend, Dr. J. Zink, *Upbringing:
Raising Emotionally Intelligent Children,* to get the best
advice I know on the subject of being a Mom or Dad. In his
book, J. answers 52 questions that he has been asked most
often in his career as a therapist. J. has written six other

books that would do you well to read. They are entitled *Building Positive Self-Concept in Kids* (1981), *Motivating Kids* (1983), *Ego States* (1986), *Dearly Beloved: Secrets of Successful Marriage* (1988), *The Parent Your Parents Were Not* (1990), and *Face It: A Spiritual Journey of Leadership* (1996) — co-authored with Ray Anderson and myself.

I know from my own experience that there is one very important trait that almost all people recognize in others, and that is sincerity. Somehow, we just know if people are sincere or not, don't we? This is true regardless of one's education, economic status, or in many cases, even language.

When I was a sophomore in college, I was struggling with defining my major. My father was a very successful dentist. Since he was my first role model, I somehow just assumed that I should be a dentist, because he provided a great standard of living for our family and seemed to really enjoy his profession.

Down deep in my heart, I suspected that I would never be a good dentist because I didn't have the patience, which meant I would more than likely never have the patients. I also did not like the thought of being confined to the detail that the profession required. I was searching for someone to help me with my dilemma when I was fortunate to meet Dr. Bob Hamm, professor of marketing in the College of Business at Oklahoma State University. At that time, I was still enrolled in the College of Arts and Sciences.

The minute I met Dr. Hamm, I knew that he cared about people, and he was radiant in his desire to help me select a career path. After our initial conversation, he suggested I switch to the College of Business. Even though he barely knew me, he took the time to ask me a few questions and take a sincere interest in me, for which I will be forever thankful to him.

During the second semester of my sophomore year, I was fortunate to have Dr. Hamm as my professor for an entry level marketing course. Midway through the semester, Dr. Hamm stopped me in the hall of the College of Business one day and said, "Charlie, you're going to be a great marketing man." I said, "I am? Sounds good to me." The additional interest and confidence he showed in me that day was a gift that really boosted my self-confidence toward staying in the College of Business. This brings to mind another one of my favorite sayings, which is, "The past is history, the future is a mystery, the moment is a gift, and that's why we call it the present."[10]

Dr. Hamm took a sincere interest in me during that important part of my life, and to this day, he is a mentor and role model to me and hundreds of other students whom he has encountered along the way.

Thanks for the present, Bob.

Ten years ago this year, I met Gordon Whitener, who was 25 years old at the time. Gordon was the head of recruiting for the football program at Oklahoma State

---

[10] Unknown

University. The minute I met Gordon, I knew that he was a born leader and someone I wanted to be associated with, professionally and personally. Today, he runs our largest division, Interface Americas, with sales in excess of $700 million.

During our friendship over the last ten years, I have mentored Gordon and tried to be a good role model. This has been a pretty tough assignment because he is a role model as well, with very high standards. In fact, he often becomes my mentor and role model — a very interesting role reversal.

Gordon played a major role in recruiting Barry Sanders into the football program at Oklahoma State in 1986. Barry only had three scholarships offered to him: one to Wichita State, one to University of Tulsa, and the other to Oklahoma State. Most of the scouts thought he was too short. As most sports fans know, Barry Sanders went on to break every rushing record at OSU, won the Heisman Trophy and today is arguably the best running back in the history of the National Football League.

Because of my friendship with Gordon and my involvement at Oklahoma State, I had the opportunity to meet Barry a couple of times when he was playing at OSU. My son, Chuck, an All-City lineman for Lovett High School in Atlanta, Georgia his senior year, absolutely loves football. Barry Sanders has been one of Chuck's heroes since he first met him when he was 10 years old. When the

Heisman Trophy was awarded in 1988, Chuck and I watched the ceremony on TV with great anticipation, hoping that Barry would win so we could have braggin' rights and to be able to say, "We know Barry Sanders."

When Barry won the Heisman, he set a new standard of humility, almost refusing to be singled out as a hero. His humility really impressed many people, and especially Chuck. To this day, Chuck's room is covered with posters of Barry Sanders.

Two years ago, the Detroit Lions (Barry's team) played the Atlanta Falcons here in Atlanta. Chuck begged Gordon to figure out some way for us to get to see Barry. The security was tight, and even Gordon couldn't get to him; however, we did get close enough to the team's bus as they were boarding after the game for Gordon to yell, "Hey Barry, it's Gordon." Barry stopped, turned around, and walked straight to the three of us. He remembered Chuck and me from past get-togethers at Oklahoma State. We were in awe. We had a short conversation, and Chuck was pumped. He could hardly wait to get home and tell his friends that he saw Barry again.

Barry is the ultimate role model of professional athletes because he recognizes the impact he can have on others, particularly young people. He realizes the importance of what other people think of him; and not because of any self proclamation of professionalism.

Another profound mentoring moment in time occurred

when our company celebrated the beginning of our 25th year in business. We held a global gathering of 1,100 people at the Grand Wailea Resort in Maui, Hawaii in April of 1997. I was responsible for planning this world-wide gathering, which took two years to orchestrate. Needless to say, this was a very busy but exciting week, during which I made over 25 presentations.

Even though this event was held during the school year, all the Eitel children were able to attend the majority of the meeting. I guess this was the first time they realized what I do for a living. Stephanie, who is a senior at Southern Methodist University in Dallas, had to return to school two days before the closing ceremony to avoid missing too many classes. When I awoke on the morning of her departure I found the following note under my door. I would like to share it with you. As a role model it is sometimes hard to know how good of a job you are doing, but for me this letter says it all.

April 9, 1997

DAD,

    I wanted to write you a note, not to brown nose or toot your horn, but to tell you that what you have done for me cannot even be expressed in words. You are such an amazing leader. I can't tell you how good it has made me feel to be your daughter. This meeting has shown me what a powerful impact you have made, not only in your company, but also in the world. It fascinates me to see how your company incorporates itself with the environment. As you know, the mountains, the sky, the beautiful green earth, all things created by God give me a sense of freedom and spirituality. Without those things, I would be lost. It gives me comfort that 1,100 others are as committed to saving this earth as I am. You make me proud to be an "Eitel". You make me proud to even be <u>linked</u> to Interface. I love you dad, not only for being a wonderful father, but also for the perfect example you have set for your employees. I love you! Can't wait to see you at the end of school.

Love always,
Stephanie

P.S. You ARE THE BEST!!!

ESTABLISHING RAPPORT

VI

Everyone in a leadership position needs to learn to let go of their position power and establish rapport by shifting their style from that of boss to coach.

AS PART OF planning our world meeting last year in Hawaii, I had the opportunity to get to know all the speakers and entertainers. Through my friendship with Tom Crum, I had the pleasure of getting to meet the late John Denver. John has always been one of my heroes, so it was a real honor for me to meet him.

In January 1997, the planning committee for the World Meeting held a session near John's home in Monterey, California. In conjunction with this meeting we invited John and Tom to join us for a few hours. Our committee spent most of the morning working through all sorts of logistical issues so that we could have the afternoon free to spend with Tom and John. They arrived around 2:00, after a round of golf. We spent an hour or so getting to know each other and modeling out what *establishing rapport* is all about. Going around the table, we each took a turn sharing with the group something about ourselves that would help us get to know one another. When it came John's turn, he said, "Hi, I'm John Denver. I'm a song writer and a singer. I am also an environmentalist, and I love what you guys are doing to help save our planet. Now, how can I help?"

We kicked around all sorts of thoughts during the following two hours, and ended up with some great ideas. We later learned that John was really nervous about meeting with our group. It may have been because Tom Crum gave us such a glowing reference and introduction. The funny thing is that John, the international celebrity, was more nervous about meeting us than we were about meeting him.

As it turned out, John was so moved by our vision and mission that he decided to write a song for our meeting (possibly his last one), entitled, "Blue Water World." He performed the song the morning of our closing ceremony on April 10, 1997. This was his gift to Interface and his endorsement of our push toward becoming a sustainable corporation.

Prior to John's death in October 1997, we spoke on several occasions, and I believe we were headed toward a special friendship that I think would have lasted a lifetime.

Anyone who knew John quickly realized that he *marched to his own drummer,* and that his songs reflected his inner soul. He had a way of establishing a rapport with his music that led you to his vision. During one of our last conversations, I specifically remember John pointing out that he had finally learned that he could not control other people; but rather only influence them, which he clearly did with some of the most powerful and meaningful words ever set to music.

The following excerpt from *Please Understand Me*[11] is a good starting point for all of us who want to work harder to establish rapport with others, and would have made a great song for John Denver.

Different Drums and Different Drummers

If I do not want what you want,
please try not to tell me that my want is wrong.

Or if I believe other than you,
at least pause before you correct my view.

Or if my emotion is less than yours,
or more, given the same circumstances,
try not to ask me to feel more strongly or weakly.

Or yet if I act, or fail to act,
in the manner of your design for action,
let me be.

---

[11] David Kelrsey and Marilyn Bates

I do not, for the moment at least,
ask you to understand me.
That will come only when you are willing
to give up changing me into a copy of you.

I may be your spouse, your parent,
your offspring, your friend, or your colleague.
If you will allow me any of my wants,
or emotions, or beliefs, or actions,
then you open yourself,
so that some day these ways of mine
might not seem so wrong,
and might finally appear to you as right - for me.

To put up with me is the first step to understanding me.
Not that you embrace my ways as right for you,
but that you are no longer irritated or disappointed
with me for my seeming waywardness.

And in understanding me
you might come to prize my differences
from you, and, far from seeking to change me,
preserve and even nurture those differences.

After reading this poem I hope it will help you realize that the world does not revolve around the self. To prove my point, go to the store and buy a map of the world, and you will find the continent of the country where you bought it to be in the center of the map.

This wake-up call first occurred to me in September 1996, when I had the opportunity and honor to participate in a three day experiential learning *Play to Win*[12] session with our Interface Europe leadership team in southern France. As I walked into the room where we were meeting, I noticed a map on the wall with Europe right in the center of the world. It may have been my imagination, but it even seemed like France was depicted as being larger than it actually is.

All written maps are inaccurate and incomplete in that they relay the landscape from the best information available.

Speaking of inaccurate maps, that's exactly what I was faced with during my three days with our European leadership team. Quite frankly, I did not realize the diversity and power of the many cultures of Europe.

A few years earlier, I had an opportunity to spend a week at the London School of Business in conjunction with an organization I am a member of, The Society of International Business Fellows (SIBF). I remember listening to one of our keynote speakers describe his perception of the difference between heaven and hell, using a few European countries to make his point. I'll never forget what he said. It goes like this.

---

[12] Play to Win is a registered trademark of Pecos River® Division, Aon Consulting, Inc.

HEAVEN IS:	HELL IS:
BRITISH PUBS	BRITISH CHEFS
FRENCH CHEFS	FRENCH ENGINEERS
GERMAN ENGINEERS	GERMAN PUBS
ITALIAN LOVERS	ITALIAN ORGANIZERS
SWISS ORGANIZERS	SWISS LOVERS

During our three day session, my education on heaven and hell barely scratched the surface toward my understanding and appreciation of the diversity of our associates who reside in Europe, and for that matter, all over the world. Through the help of our facilitators, Michael Lonergan, Allison Helstrup, and John Wenburg, we completed a watershed *hook-up* event that proved to me that all cultures can establish rapport and gain in-depth appreciation for each other.

During our stay in southern France, it became crystal clear to me the importance of *hooking-up our company, worldwide.* (More on this subject in Chapter Ten.)

Like most corporations, we conduct regular business reviews at our various businesses around the world. This activity is a key part of my job that I really enjoy, because it gives me a chance to interact with our people, face to face. Many corporate leaders, who are in a similar role of *position power,* view the same type of meeting as an opportunity to *beat people up.* They actually believe that they can motivate people by embarrassing them in front of their peers. I know this is true because I have worked for miserable people like this, who enjoy putting people down in public to *remind everyone who is boss*. We have a few competitors who are masters of this military type activity, which, in my view, goes a long way toward explaining why we are rapidly growing our business and developing our people and they are not.

My job requires me to be available and approachable. By supporting my associates, I have a better chance of serving them by learning the truth regarding what is right and wrong in our business, versus creating an environment where they are afraid to share the cold, hard facts for fear of retribution.

Everyone in a leadership position needs to learn to *let go* of their position power and establish rapport by shifting their style from that of *boss* to *coach*.

Dr. J. Zink once told me, "There is no such thing as *constructive criticism*, only *criticism*."

After World War II, most leaders around the world believed that what people wanted most was security (common sense would indicate they did), so organizations believed that money was the answer. Then in the 60's and 70's, people said, "What we really want is growth and development." The buzzword of that era was *leadership,* which companies tried to provide. Now, we realize what people want most is *meaning* and *purpose* in their lives.

To achieve this, leaders must do one simple thing — they must *sincerely care*.

If you are in a position to influence others and earn their respect, you must first learn to listen to them in order for them to believe that you care.

One of the most difficult aspects of my job is knowing that most of our 7,500 associates worldwide know who I am, but I do not know all of them. A few years ago, I learned to accept this stressful fact and decided that my only salvation is an approach I call "The Power of One." Here's how it works. I decided to give 100% of my focus and attention to the people I am able to interact with at each of our locations, and let go of the disappointment that I cannot know everyone who works for us. If I am walking through one of our plants or offices and meet someone who shows interest in talking to me, I do my very best to give them 100% of my attention on the spot. I feel that if I can exert sufficient influence on him or her, it will proliferate to others in the organization. I do not want to be viewed as some sort of a glad-hander, walking around like a politician, shaking hands with everyone without making eye contact and taking time to try to get to know them as individuals.

I *sincerely* care about all of our associates and I do the best I can to let them know it.

EARNING RESPECT

VII

*Leaders must only say things
that are true and say them
with consistency.*

ACCORDING TO my friend, Mildred Ramsey, people need
recognition, respect and reinforcement. She should know,
because at 73 years old, Mildred has become quite famous
for her heroic stand against the union organization efforts
that occurred at the J. P. Stevens textile plants in South
Carolina some 20 years ago. Today, she is one of the most
sought after speakers by companies in the United States
that want to hear her stories on how to create the kind of
work environment where people are happy and productive.

Everyone needs recognition, even if they don't know
they need it. I'm not necessarily talking about public
recognition, even though many people love this kind of
attention as well. More often, people want to be recognized
and appreciated by the people they work with, and
specifically, their boss (that is, if they respect their boss).
In one of Mildred's recent speeches to our employees, she
pointed out that *the people on the shop floor really*

appreciate Interface's leadership team, but to them, their supervisor is just as important and, quite frankly, more important than upper management, because this is the individual with whom they have a daily relationship.

After all, when they have a problem with a sick child, a death in the family, or some other traumatic experience, their supervisor is the one they need to be able to rely on for support and understanding. Mildred said, "When my husband died, the big dogs came to the funeral and I really appreciated that, but I was looking for my supervisor, and he was there, along with my co-workers, and I'll never forget it!" This was clearly one of the key reasons why Mildred Ramsey took a stand for J. P. Stevens against an unnecessary union drive in the late 70's.

People are professionals because of what other people think of them, not because of any self proclamation of professionalism. I don't remember Mildred's supervisor's name, but she does, because to her, he was the president of J. P. Stevens. In Mildred's humorous talks, she usually asks the question, "Who do you think I missed the most when they were not at work, the janitor or the president?" Since we know presidents don't clean rest rooms, I suspect you know the answer.

Earning the respect of the people we work with is critically important regardless of their particular function. Respect always follows good habits. "Make good habits and they will follow you."[13]

---

[13] Park Cousins

Striving to make good habits, in early 1995, our company, Interface, declared a "war on waste." This initiative is focused on eliminating the concept of waste; not just waste itself. In the airline industry, no one budgets how many planes they plan to crash. Their target is zero, and anything short of this goal will likely result in costs which usually include the loss of human life. Yet in business, we intentionally plan to fail through budgeting waste.

At Interface, we are on a mission to become a sustainable corporation through our QUEST/EcoSense® revolution. QUEST (every company should have a few acronyms) stands for *Quality Utilizing Employee Suggestions and Teamwork*. Through our EcoSense and QUEST initiatives, we are vitally interested in learning all that we can about what is right and wrong in our business. We have created an environment where our people feel free to tell us the good things that are going on so that we can celebrate and replicate these activities around the world. We are just as interested in the non-value added activities so we can eradicate them. We define waste as, "Any measurable cost that goes into our product or service that does not come out as value to our customers." Over the last three years, we have taken $50 million in measurable waste out of our company, by listening to four groups — those making, counting, selling and buying our products and services. We respect what they have to say and we are acting on their advice every moment of the day.

We have over 400 QUEST teams in place and working all over the world, centered on what our people think is important. The people who are actually doing the work are best qualified to make decisions on what needs to be changed to achieve zero waste and sustainability.

"If you make your job important, it is likely to return the favor."[14] Our people have made their jobs important because our leadership team has made sure that they know they are the life blood of everything the company does, and that we sincerely care about each and every one of them. To help facilitate this type of culture we work very hard to do everything possible to be sure we don't create a class separation among the various levels of responsibility of our associates.

As I mentioned earlier, we celebrated the beginning of the 25th anniversary of our company last year at the Grand Wailea Resort in Maui, Hawaii. Even though a substantial portion of the cost of this event was funded by our suppliers, we couldn't have all of our associates participate, and we were faced with a potential morale problem in deciding exactly which employees should be invited. We had budgeted for 1,000 people (including personnel from sales, marketing, manufacturing, our technical staff, product development, finance, legal, etc.) to attend. We did not plan to invite anyone from the shop floor of our manufacturing plants.

Gordon Whitener and his team came up with an idea

[14] Unknown

that solved this tough issue. We decided to invite 50 people from our plants around the world via a lottery. Each business unit was offered a pro rata number of meeting slots, based on their sales as a percentage of the corporation as a whole. For example, a division with $100 million in sales qualified to send five people (one-tenth of the 50 slots), since at that time our overall sales were $1.0 billion. In the drawing, each employee was afforded one chance to attend the meeting for each year's service to the company. Twenty-five years with the company equaled 25 chances, so the associates with the most tenure had a greater opportunity to win.

As you might expect, we had 50 additional, very happy people attend our meeting. This fair approach to a difficult problem totally diffused any ill will and potential politics. Their attendance also went a long way toward providing for a more diverse meeting. These 50 associates became delegates representing our whole company — what a powerful addition they were.

Politics will ruin a company and I want no part of any such activity. Had we not come up with a fair approach to this sensitive issue, we clearly would have been setting the stage for a *have/have not* scenario.

I honestly believe we have very little, if any, politics at Interface because this type of behavior is not rewarded. Every now and then we end up with a politician, but when they learn that there is no one to politic with, they leave.

In the book, *The Discipline of Market Leaders* by Treacy and Wiersema, they point out that every company tends to excel at one of three core competencies: 1) operational excellence; 2) product leadership; and 3) customer intimacy. All companies would like to claim that they are good at all three, and I feel no different about Interface. When forced to rank our core competencies, I must admit that we are a customer intimate company; but, we first focus on our employees as the key to being sure that we are customer intimate. We know that if we treat our people right, they will treat our customers right. Besides, it's the right thing to do, and is consistent with our mission to create an environment free from politics.

Companies that view themselves as customer intimate are quite different from those who believe their core competency is operational excellence or product leadership. At Interface, I am confident we have the best products, styled and designed by the best of the best. But when it's all said and done, I'm convinced that our current success is more about the quality of our people and their relationships with our customers.

As I said earlier, my job is to help create an environment where our people want to get up and go to work in the morning, and where Interface is the kind of company other companies want to do business with. I call this working on the *top side of the business.* Any person in a position of authority can cut costs. This activity takes no special acumen or leadership; just the stroke of a pen. Some companies are eager to refer to these programs as *lean*, but they are really *mean*.

My role is to focus on growing our business by being sure that we have the best quality, service, delivery and products, and most importantly, intimate customer relationships. Then our customers will buy from us at a price that enables us to provide benefits to our employees, and an outstanding return to our shareholders.

I believe that the customer is always right, but not everyone is a customer. This concept became clear to me several years ago when I met Larry Steinmetz. Larry owns his own company, "High Yield Management," based in Boulder, Colorado. He taught me something I will never forget. He said, "You signal how much respect you have for your product or service when you quote your price." He clearly believes that people buy on price — high price, not low price. He is right, and if you ever hear him speak, you will become a believer too. Our customers are being asked to know more than ever before about the products and services that they purchase. The reality is that they simply do not have the time and resources available to make intelligent decisions about the true value of a product or service, because there are so many variables presented by so many sales people claiming to have the *best stuff*.

If your customers trust you (and I believe ours trust us), then price is only one of the components that leads to complete satisfaction. Companies that sell on price (high volume and low price) die on price, and unfortunately, their employees die with them. Managers often think they are very clever in eliminating jobs and beating up their suppliers, to win business by lowering their costs and being able to sell on price. They later learn that this ridiculous formula will guarantee failure over the long term. We want our associates to be well paid and for our suppliers to make a fair profit on us. Why not? Anything short of this way of thinking represents a lack of leadership. Quote the price that your product is worth.

Every leader has a responsibility to ensure the economic sustainability of their enterprise, and they need to be sure that all costs, including payroll, are within the parameters of reality and market conditions. We all must be careful to keep an eye on costs and not act like Santa Claus or we may end up pulling a sleigh.

Great companies know they must provide the best product, service, quality, and delivery, and nurture customer relationships, to be entitled to sell at unit prices above their competition. There will always be competitors in the market place, selling on low price and using *smoke and mirrors* to confuse buyers, but they rarely, if ever, make it over the long haul. Remember that if you sell on price, you are likely to end up in that horrible down sizing dilemma that many companies force themselves into. What customers and employees want is to be treated fairly, and with respect, sincerity and honesty. This is why leaders must only say things that are true and say them consistently.

RESOLVING CONFLICT

VIII

*Trouble is inevitable;
misery is optional.*

LAST YEAR, I had the opportunity to meet Yvon Chouinard,
the founder of Patagonia. Our Chairman, Ray Anderson,
was invited to speak at their annual suppliers' conference,
and as a result, I was invited to tag along. Randy Harward,
Director of Quality and Environmental Affairs of
Patagonia, also had heard about Ray's vision to lead
Interface toward sustainability.

During the course of the conference, Yvon addressed
the entire group. He opened his presentation by announc-
ing to us that he really did not like business, but had
discovered that it was a way for him to earn enough money
to be able to enjoy what he loves most, which is surfing and
climbing. Even though he is Chairman of the Board at
Patagonia, he spends most of his time developing new
products. Patagonia makes fantastic products that are
designed for specific technical uses. In his presentation, he
asked the audience, "Does anyone know why people
climb?" After a lengthy period of silence, he gave his answer.

He said, "You know there isn't anything up there. The reason people climb is to get to know themselves and therefore resolve their internal conflicts."

The reason I began this chapter by referencing Yvon's speech is because I am convinced that we must all resolve past conflicts. I spoke earlier about the importance of understanding one's own story.

One of the first steps toward resolving conflict is to let go of what you can't control. In the book, *The Corporate Mystic* by Hendricks and Ludeman, they point out that there are four things we can't control: 1) the feelings and emotions of other people; 2) anything that has already happened; 3) anything that has not yet happened; and 4) what goes on inside our bodies. While we can influence people's emotions, the future and what goes on inside our bodies, we can't control these events.

When I heard my friend, Mildred Ramsey, speak earlier this year, she said something that really struck me. "Trouble is inevitable; misery is optional." Many people are miserable because they have yet to resolve past conflicts in their lives. Freud said, "Secrets make you sick." I don't know who penned the following quote, but I love it. "The truth shall set me free, but first it will make me miserable."

Resolving conflict is all about the truth.

Dr. J. Zink knows and teaches that behind depression there is always anger. Anger often stems from conflict within ourselves and with others. There are many people who believe they are victims of bad luck, and there is no doubt that many people incur more than their fair share of bad luck; however, these individuals represent a small part of our western population. For the most part, we create our own luck through choices. I like to hire people with long strings of good luck. Good luck is almost always a result of good choices.

People do fall on bad luck from time to time, e.g., unexpected illness or being involved in accidents; however, the reality is we can do a lot to influence our luck. Some friends of mine recently lost one of their teenage children in an automobile accident where alcohol was involved. This was bad luck that followed a bad choice; but when a tragedy like this hits close to home, it's human nature to feel victimized.

Throughout life, we are continuously forced to deal with the unexpected. My friend, Tom Crum, teaches Aikido, a martial art, to demonstrate the power of *blending energy* when conflict arises, as contrasted with our typical reaction, which is to fight or resist conflict. According to Tom, "utilizing Aikido, we are given a gift of energy in which neither side loses." Resolving conflict is rarely about who is right; it is about acknowledgment and appreciation of differences. Therefore when we encounter a dose of bad luck, we must learn to move into the conflict and accept the cards we are dealt, blending our energy with the problem; thus, actually using the bad luck as an asset or a tool to create a new opportunity for good luck.

In the past few months, we have retained ©Talent+®, a company based in Lincoln, Nebraska, to help us assess why certain people in our company perform better in some areas than others. Talent+ conducts an interview process in which they try to understand people in nine categories, one being *response to negativity*. According to Bea Haney, who interviewed me, I tested off the chart in this area. *Off the chart* means that no matter what negative news I am given, I will keep asking questions to dissect this information until I can find a realistic, positive option, and thus get things headed back in the right direction. I'm happy to say that I *never* view myself as a victim. I am thankful for this trait, even though I'm not sure where it came from. But I suspect I learned it before I was five or six years old!

Tom Crum says, "Conflict is just an interference pattern with energy." Bad luck or bad news is no different. Tom states in his book, *The Magic of Conflict*, "Nature uses conflict as a primary motivator for change."

My friend, Larry Wilson, describes change as potentially occurring in three ways: 1) through crisis; 2) through evolution; and 3) through anticipation. At first glance, you may think that changing through crisis is the worst possible way to change. Actually, a crisis has its benefits because time is always valuable and there is a tendency for immediate action necessary to turn the situation around.

The most unproductive way to change is through

evolution. We describe evolutionary change as changing incrementally or so slowly that such change is barely noticeable. Little personal growth occurs through evolutionary change. The third and most effective way to change is through *anticipation.* Changing through anticipation requires vision, which is achievable by going through the steps I described in Chapter One.

At Interface we often use a *SWOT* (strengths, weaknesses, opportunities and threats) approach to help continuously re-create our future. We do this through a brainstorming process in which we identify four or five major issues or subjects that are specifically relevant to what we are trying to become. Then using a *post-it note* approach, we randomly post thoughts of what we believe our strengths, weaknesses, opportunities and threats are, relative to that issue. We then combine all of these short phrases (one or two words) into paragraphs that state what we believe we can become. As I stated earlier, we call this, "Creating the company that, if it existed, would put us out of business."

Change can be painful, but at Interface, we find it is worth the effort every time.

No matter what kind of results you are achieving in your personal life and in your career, you can get better results, but you must change something.

Over the past several years, I have developed what I refer to as "The Ten Disciplines of Business Turnaround," which has helped guide me and my team through continuous change. No matter what business you may be involved with, I believe you will find these disciplines will work for you. You may have to change a few words here and there; however, these initiatives are so simple I believe anyone can understand, modify, and implement them.

THE TEN DISCIPLINES OF BUSINESS TURNAROUND

1. MAKE A PERMANENT COMMITMENT TO EMPLOYEE TRAINING AND EDUCATION.
2. CREATE AN ENVIRONMENT WHERE EVERY ASSOCIATE WILL WANT TO BE INVOLVED IN A WORK TEAM, FOCUSED ON WASTE REDUCTION, QUALITY IMPROVEMENT AND ENVIRONMENTAL STEWARDSHIP.
3. HOLD PRODUCT AND/OR PLANNING MEETINGS WITH ALL DIVISIONS OF THE BUSINESS ON A WEEKLY BASIS FOR ONE YEAR, AND SEMI-MONTHLY THEREAFTER.
4. LEARN TO CONTINUALLY RE-ENGINEER PRODUCTS, FOCUSED ON A GOAL OF ZERO WASTE.
5. LEARN HOW TO ACHIEVE MAXIMUM PRODUCT OUTPUT FROM THE FEWEST NUMBER OF FEEDER INPUTS.
6. DEMAND JIT (JUST IN TIME) SERVICE FROM YOUR SUPPLIERS (PARTNERS).
7. VIEW INVENTORY AS A LIABILITY, NOT AN ASSET.
8. LEARN TO "MAKE TO ORDER" (MASS CUSTOMIZATION) AND DELIVER YOUR PRODUCTS FASTER THAN ANY COMPETITOR.
9. SEGMENT TOP SELLING (PROVEN) PRODUCTS AND OFFER

IMMEDIATE SERVICE ON THIS PORTION OF YOUR BUSINESS, WHICH SHOULD REPRESENT AT LEAST 25% OF YOUR TOTAL SALES.

10. COMMUNICATE EVERYTHING YOU CAN MEASURE TO EVERYONE IN THE BUSINESS ON A REGULAR BASIS.

By having guidelines that everyone can understand, you reduce possible confusion and stress in your organization and therefore keep conflict to a minimum.

It is nice to have maps like the ten disciplines that we can continually hold up to our associates as a guideline for where we are heading. We must also continue to provide an environment where people can grow and develop every day, which is best provided through a culture free of fear.

Speaking of development, did you ever stop and think about why people go to college? The obvious answer is "to get a degree." No doubt, this is the expected outcome, but we really go to college for four reasons: 1) confidence; 2) competence; 3) character; and 4) connections. Earning a college degree today usually grants you admission to the game, and that's about all. When someone joins our company, we try to expand his or her learning from college or high school to include: 5) creativity; 6) communication skills; 7) charisma; and most importantly, 8) compatibility with other associates. Compatibility is best achieved by giving others the benefit of the doubt through support, not criticism. *Support* is the key word that helps develop a corporate culture that is wholesome and free from destructive conflict.

As I mentioned, changing through crisis is not always bad. When I joined Interface Flooring Systems in late 1993, things were not going well. At that time, IFS's sales were about $120 million, representing about one fifth of our total corporate revenue. The business was operating at around break-even. My associate, Gordon Whitener, and I had our hands full in our attempt to re-engineer and turn around the division. There were days when it seemed we had made a mistake leaving the comfortable environment of our previous employer. In February 1994 (approximately 90 days after our arrival), Gordon, who was then Senior Vice President of Sales and Marketing of Interface Flooring Systems (currently President and CEO of Interface Americas), decided to call a press conference in New York. The purpose was to meet with various trade publications, in order to share our vision for the future.

We stayed at the Grand Hyatt on 42nd Street, which is located in the center of midtown.

We were sound asleep on the 44th floor of the Grand Hyatt when the fire alarm sounded at around 2:00 a.m. I assumed it was a false alarm, but since I was located on the 44th floor, I decided it was worth opening my door and taking a quick look. As I peeked out the door, I saw that the hallway was full of smoke, and as you might expect, I said, "Oh, Lord!"

I immediately slipped on a pair of pants and a shirt and headed for Gordon's room to be sure he was awake. We must have attempted to alert each other at about the same time through different hallways. A few minutes later we found each other in the lobby of the hotel, after descending 44 flights of stairs. The lobby was full of a quite diverse group of people who looked like they were going to a Halloween party. Everything in the hotel was closed, including the bar; however, there were a couple of unoccupied sofas adjacent to the lobby. Gordon took one and I took the other. As we laid there with our hands behind our heads, I asked Gordon, "What in the world are we doing here?" After an hour or so of feeling sorry for ourselves and rehashing all the problems that we had inherited at Interface, I said, "How are we going to get out of this mess?" At the very moment I asked Gordon that question, I was reminded of the movie, "Butch Cassidy and the Sundance Kid," where Robert Redford and Paul Newman were cornered by bandits in an adobe, somewhere in Bolivia. If you saw the movie, you may recall they were asking each other the same question. Since they had no other option, they came out shooting and both were shot and killed.

Gordon's answer to my question was, "The only way out is to just fix it," and that was what we did. Thank goodness, we lived to tell the story.

Last year, Interface Flooring Systems' sales were $200

million, and we posted an operating income of $27 million. Our total corporate sales were $1,135 million, with an operating income of almost $100 million. The market value of the company has increased from $200 million to over $1.0 billion.

A lot has changed at Interface, and all for the better. Today, we truly have a company that is full of love and support, and free from destructive conflict.

UNDERSTANDING SUSTAINABILITY

IX

*The better the idea,
the more resistance you are
likely to stir up.*

THERE IS A BIG difference between deciding to jump and actually jumping. In late 1994, our Chairman, Ray Anderson, decided to jump *and jump he did,* with both feet, right into leading Interface toward sustainability. He is leading, and we are all working as fast as we can to keep up with his world changing vision, which is to make Interface the *first name* in *industrial ecology.* This sounds like a pretty ambitious goal since, according to *Fortune* magazine, Interface is the 949th largest corporation in America. How could it be possible that a commercial interiors company could even dream such a goal?

Three and one-half years have passed since Ray made this bold statement, and who knows, we may *already* be *the first name in industrial ecology.* If we're not, someone needs to tell me who is. Last year, Ray was named Co-Chair of the President's Council on Sustainable Development, a responsibility he takes seriously, and to prove it, he has made over 100 speeches on the subject in the last twelve months.

Because of his vision and mission, we have encountered our fair share of resistance and even criticism, particularly from a few competitors, but we just keep moving forward. The better the idea, the more resistance you are likely to stir up.

At about the same time Ray was creating his vision to make Interface an environmentally sustainable enterprise, we were in the process of launching a zero waste revolution at Interface called "QUEST," which I spoke about earlier. We decided to compete with perfection, and that's why QUEST is a *zero* waste based initiative.

Our push toward sustainability is a zero waste based initiative as well, except that in striving to achieve sustainability, one is still permitted to waste nonrenewable resources provided such waste is offset by restorative activities. We believe we can become a sustainable corporation, and as soon as we do, our new goal will be to become restorative. It sounds like a lofty dream for a material intensive company such as ours, which extracted 1.2 billion pounds of organic and inorganic nonrenewable resources from the earth last year.

In our effort to explain sustainability to our suppliers, employees and customers, last year we published what we believe is the first ever Sustainability Report. In this document, we went to great length to mathematically explain (confess, if you will) what we take, make and waste. We call this mathematical measurement system EcoMetrics. In our Sustainability Report, we examine seven objectives in our drive toward sustainability, which include: 1) the elimination of waste; 2) achieve benign emissions; 3) use renewable energy; 4) close the loop on the products we design and produce; 5) use resource-efficient transportation; 6) use our influence to make people more aware and sensitive to our movement; and 7) redesign commerce by focusing on service and value versus the delivery of material.

We believe that we, ultimately, must be environmentally sustainable in order to be financially sustainable. If an enterprise is sustainable, it theoretically can go on forever. We know most companies (both small and large) fail on a regular basis. If you don't believe this is true, compare today's *Fortune 500* companies to the same group 25 years ago, and you will be amazed how few companies remain on the list. When a company fails, what happens to the retired and working employees who are depending on management's judgment to do the right thing? Who pays their pensions when the company goes out of business? In some cases - no one.

Providing top quality products and/or services is a vital part of the short and long term success of any enterprise. Wells Forte said it best, "Quality is never an accident. It is always a result of high intention, sincere effort, intelligent directors and skillful executives. It represents the wise choice among many alternatives." While I agree with this quote, I also believe that the word *quality* is often misunderstood, overused, and even *abused* by many. The reason I say abused is because you can manufacture a top quality product that conforms to the specifications and at the same time, plan (in standards) to waste certain material, labor and energy. Top quality is a result of high intention. The question is, "What are the intentions?"

Remember, "Design is a manifestation of human intention." The way we have designed and produced products in the past may have been the wise choice then, among the available alternatives. Today, we have new alternatives, which include moving toward building a sustainable and restorative enterprise. Doing the same thing over and over and expecting different results is a sign of insanity. Planning to waste nonrenewable resources over and over is a perfect example of such insanity.

Here is another way to look at the same problem on a more personal level. If you decide to retire at age 60 and know that you are going to live to be 100 (like George Burns), how much money would you need upon retirement to live the exact same lifestyle you would be living at age 60? You and I know that this is a mathematical computation that can be calculated with a high degree of accuracy. All you need to do is simply total up all forms of your financial capital at age 60, project a rate of return, add for anticipated inflation, and be sure you have enough money at death to pay your estate taxes without burdening your relatives. People make these judgments every day through the help of financial planners.

Almost everyone knows that oil is a finite, non-renewable resource and we are running out. Various experts have predicted supplies will be depleted in the next 50 to 100 years. Regardless, we are running out, just like anyone will run out of money if they fail to plan for their future. I'm not trying to scare you but this is a cold hard fact. When it comes to the environment, we are spending our retirement now. The current market price of oil is far short of reflecting the "real" price, based on its long term scarcity. It just amazes me that we are intelligent enough to produce highly accurate actuarial charts on insurance policies and pension funds, and have the ability to calculate the present value of money 100 years out, yet we can't face the truth that we are running out of nonrenewable resources. This reality is being accelerated by the fact that our world population is increasing at the rate of 80 million people per year.

In his book, *The Living Company,* the author, Arie de Geus, acknowledges four characteristics of long lived companies, which are: 1) sensitive to the environment; 2) strong sense of identity; 3) tolerant and decentralized; and 4) conservative in financing. He also states, "Frequently someone within the enterprise will identify the crisis ahead of time, but not as a crisis; it is a new opportunity, an alternative avenue for company growth and profitability." This is exactly what Ray Anderson has done, identify a new opportunity. We've labeled it, "Doing well by doing good."[15] Our financial results speak for themselves, but what is equally important is the influence we are having on our suppliers, associates and customers.

I mentioned our relationship with Patagonia earlier. They are a fine company with a lot of influence. They actually do not manufacture many products; but rather, they subcontract all of their production to commission producers. Until we got to know our friends at Patagonia, I assumed that their sales were in the billions because of their influence and well-respected brands that are so widely known. When I learned their actual sales numbers, which are much more modest than I anticipated, I was amazed at the degree of influence wielded by this company, particularly on people who are sensitive to environmental issues.

Influence is a key word that can accelerate change, and that's what Interface's move toward sustainability is all about. From our perspective, we are leading by example. And in an implied way, we are asking others, "What would be the consequences of your actions if everyone did it?"

Speaking of influence, we made an interesting discovery at Interface less than two years ago. As the world's largest and, I might add (in my unbiased view), best manufacturer

---

[15] Ray C. Anderson

of global commercial interiors products, we realized that the most important asset in the commercial workplace is the people.

Knowing the importance of the influence we have had on other companies through our sustainability movement, we decided to start our own learning company, called *one world learning*, to spread the word. Today, this new business is headed by David Black, a long time friend and seasoned teacher. Under David's leadership, we have assembled an outstanding team of facilitators. We are now leading other companies through our experiential exercises and initiatives that we have created, as well as *The Natural Step (TNS)* training, founded by Dr. Karl-Henrick Robèrt, an environmental visionary and Swedish research scientist. We were introduced to *TNS* through our friend and well-known environmentalist, Paul Hawken.

When we get involved in helping other companies, our first mission is to assist in connecting their top teams and, eventually, their entire employee base. We want to help them connect at a level that would never be possible without the *breakthrough approach* we use to *hook them up*. We focus on personal change and therefore help individuals anticipate what they can achieve with vision. We further help them in converting that vision into a bias for action in order to discover what is possible. We are not consultants in the traditional sense, and we are not trying to tell people or companies what they should be; but rather, we're helping them to realize what they can be. We help individuals and therefore the company channel human talent to the part of their organization where people are happiest and most productive.

We know that the only way we can be assured of conducting a successful *one world learning* program is to ensure we enroll the CEO. In fact, this is the only way we will get involved with a company. We must have a buy-in from the top, so we insist that the CEO jump in the fish bowl with his or her leadership team to ensure the commitment connection is made with total energy and success.

Most people can only see what they have already experienced. In our learning activities, we really don't tell you anything you don't already know, but we do hold you up to the mirror so you can see yourself differently and therefore act differently.

We may be only the 949th largest corporation in America according to *Fortune* magazine, but we are changing the way things work on this planet, and we are not turning back. *one world learning* is our vehicle to facilitate this change.

HOOKING-IT-UP

X

*When Ray said, "Hook-it-up,"
I had no idea of the magnitude of the
project that was ahead of me.*

IN OCTOBER 1994, our Chairman, Ray Anderson, asked me to play a larger role at Interface and head-up our global floorcoverings operation. At that time, our annual sales in this business segment were around $600 million. In a half kidding/half serious way, I asked him, "What do you want me to do?" He said, "Just hook-it-up." Anyone who has followed Interface in recent years knows that the rest of this story is pretty much history, because today our company is *hooked-up.* We are continually fine tuning many details, but we have come a long way toward building bridges and removing barriers among our associates worldwide.

In February 1997, I became President of Interface, Inc. I doubt this event would have happened if the Board of Directors, and specifically Ray, had not been pleased with our efficient and effective *hooking-it-up process.* I believe that our accomplishment is landmark in the commercial interiors business, and perhaps for any industry. This chapter, *Hooking-It-Up,* focuses primarily on Interface, because I really don't know of any other companies that have ever attempted such a feat with the same degree of intensity. When Ray said, "Hook-it-up," I had no idea of the magnitude of the project that was ahead of me.

For the previous ten years before my arrival, Interface had been methodically accumulating various businesses and brands around the world. By late 1994, we had carpet manufacturing plants located in Australia, Canada, England, Holland, Northern Ireland, and the United States (Cartersville, LaGrange and West Point, Georgia, and Los Angeles, California), and plans for a plant in Thailand. As of today, our Thailand plant has been up and running for two years, and we will soon have a new plant operational in Shanghai. We also recently purchased the carpet operations of Readicut International in Europe, giving us additional plants in England and in Holland. When you add our Interior Fabrics facilities (Guilford of Maine, Toltec, Intek, Camborne, and Stevens Linen), our raised floor business in Grand Rapids, Michigan, and our chemical business in Rockmart, Georgia, you will arrive at a total of 29 manufacturing plants, located in seven countries, on four continents.

As I began to understand the diversity and complexity of our company in late 1994, I decided the best thing I could do would be to focus my energy on what our worldwide businesses have in common. As the world's largest manufacturer of carpet tiles (carpet squares), it was clear that we were manufacturing our products and delivering our services in a *similar* manner. We have carpet tile plants located in Australia, Canada, China, England, Holland, Northern Ireland, Thailand, and the United States (LaGrange, Georgia) — all state-of-the-art manufacturing plants essentially making similar products.

I soon learned that *similar* and *same* are considerably different.

A few years earlier, I became quite interested in what Ford Motor Company had accomplished in building the first ever global car, the *Taurus*. They did a very logical thing. They stopped and asked their customers globally what features they were looking for in a mid-priced automobile. They were not particularly concerned about what their existing manufacturing facilities had the ability to make, but were more interested in what the global consumer was looking for in an automobile. When the results from the surveys came in, Ford realized that many of the features their customers were looking for existed in their own cars already being assembled around the world. As they continued to analyze the information from these consumer surveys, it occurred to them that they already had almost all the components for a *best in class* car; they were just not in one automobile. Ford ended up copying the best ideas from their own products and then set about to design and build the most successful and profitable automobile in their history. In the process, they had to modify their plants to *hook-it-up,* but it was worth the investment. As you probably recognize, the quality of the Taurus is fabulous, because through good communication among their manufacturing plants and design teams, they were able to lower their off-quality and waste.

The Ford Taurus became the global corporate car that many multinational companies used as standard because it represents a top value worldwide. It is also a very popular four door sedan for middle income families all over the world.

I stated earlier that we have a core value at Interface, and that is *not to duplicate or knock off our competitors' products.* In hooking-up Interface globally, we hold true to this value. Our share of the global carpet tile market is in excess of 40%, so all we had to do was to take a close look at ourselves, and we found the best in class answers. Utilizing QUEST as our global standard for measuring waste, we were able to quickly figure out who was doing the best job at particular processes. Under the leadership of David Oakey, owner of David Oakey Designs, we decided the first step was to try to source our raw materials on a global basis. DuPont is our largest supplier, so at first blush, we thought this would be a fairly easy first step. As it turned out, we were amazed at the apparent lack of communication between DuPont North America and DuPont Europe. This apparent, communication and perhaps cultural, gap turned out to be a signal for the problems we later encountered in our own *hook-up*. We literally had to force our supplier to focus on our needs as their customer and quit worrying about who in their organization was going to get the credit. They finally came around, but only in the nick of time. They almost lost a big piece of our business over what appeared to be a fairly simple, internal communication problem. It may sound like I am being critical, but I am declaring quite the opposite; because we ran into the same problem in our own company and with many of our other suppliers.

Once we were able to establish global raw materials sourcing (mainly yarn), we then set about to select global tufting machines, focused on two manufacturers with three gauges. We were moving our focus from *similar* to *same*. We then began to agree globally on the same backing technology and, eventually, every detail as to how we build our products. Much like Ford, our waste was dramatically reduced, our cycle time in manufacturing went from an average of seven weeks to less than three weeks, our costs came down, and as you would expect, our margins went up.

Today, we have the ability to make the exact same products with the same yarns, machines, dye methods, and backing technology, globally. The short term benefits have been many, but the halo effects are even greater. We have a built-in disaster plan enabling us to shift production from one plant to another, a benefit that is invisible to our customers, but one that gives us a lot of flexibility to meet their needs. We can shift production from plant to plant in order to balance capacities and even hedge currencies. But most important of all, we can *sell* globally. None of our competitors come close to our global capabilities. Today we are manufacturing over 100 colors of carpet tile globally and selling these products to approximately 200 multinational customers.

When we were planning this *hook-up* almost four years ago, I believed if we could accomplish this initiative, there would be no global competition, and there isn't. What we have been through is tough and expensive, but well worth the effort because we now sell, manufacture and deliver our products globally. It really does not benefit you to be a global company unless there is a direct benefit to your employees, customers and shareholders.

Even though we are the world's low cost producer of carpet tile (which clearly has been a benefit of hooking-up), what's more important is that our customers trust us to advise them on exactly what products and services they need so they, too, can establish global standards.

While the *hook-up* of manufacturing plants was taking place, we were also quietly putting together a global account sales team that was focused on account based selling rather than geographical based selling. Today, we have 1,100 people in sales and marketing worldwide and have hand-picked 45 account managers to fill this important role. They are *hooked-up,* as well, through the web and connected via our main computer network server. They share real time information daily about what is going on with our 200 targeted multinational customers. We are building a worldwide data base that we believe will enable us to grow into our name, *Interface*. More specifically, we plan to allow other companies to access our global information *hook-up,* which may well result in further acquisitions, joint ventures or alliances.

Our biggest obstacle in selling globally is that most of our customers don't know how to buy globally. Many people are attempting to sell worldwide, but they don't deliver the *best in class* products. We are the trailblazer and will not give up on this initiative because it is a better deal for our customers.

Most of us never recognize opportunity until it goes to work in one of our competitors' companies. I believe our *hook-it-up effort* will enable us to continue to gain market share worldwide, and is a clear competitive advantage.

Today, I describe Interface as a centralized attempt to diversify and decentralize the global operations, and at the same time, keep it hooked-up. Think about that point for a while.

During the week of April 6, 1997, we conducted perhaps the most successful corporate meeting ever held in the world. In recognition of our accomplishment, we were awarded "The Global Paragon Award" by Meeting Professionals International, a global organization of professional meeting planners. This is the highest award given annually by MPI.

When I received the award on behalf of Interface in January 1998, the chairman of the selection committee told me, "It wasn't even close; you won hands down." This wonderful acknowledgment proved to me that you can accomplish anything you want to if you can dream and articulate a process to achieve a vision.

As people arrived at the meeting from the airport, we took an individual instant photo of them as they stepped off the bus, and used those photos to create a *legacy wall* that was placed outside our main meeting room. We asked each attendee to think of one thing he or she could do to help make the world a better place as a result of this *Power of One pledge* or *legacy*. After the meeting, we published a newsletter for all our employees, which included these legacies from our 1,100 attendees from 34 countries around the world. What a powerful list of legacies!

When I was in England the following September, I was presented with a letter from Dr. Ofelia Kamp. Ofelia is a medical doctor and dentist from Romania; however, she works as an account manager for Interface, because she can provide a better living for her family by working for us rather than in medicine. As you can read from her letter, which follows, she decided that her legacy was to convince the art community in Romania to paint for free to help the aging population in Romania. The country is in such a terrible financial condition that the government does not have the money to fund senior citizens' pensions. Ofelia had an artist paint two oil paintings each of our Chairman, Ray Anderson, and me. Of course, we contributed to the cause. What an appropriate story to symbolize the power and diversity of our people globally and the power of one person's legacy.

Following is Ofelia's letter to Ray Anderson, John Walker and me:

Interface Flooring bv
Industrielaan 15   Bank
P.O. Box 16   ABN-AMRO 55 30 31 325
3925 ZG Scherpenzeel
The Netherlands
Telephone: (31)3497 - 56 56   Trade register at
Telefax: (31)3497 - 83 83   Arnhem nr. 34838

Interface

Bucharest, July 1997

Dear RAY, CHARLIE and JOHN,

I start this letter, addressed to you, knowing that a new chapter opened in my life, and a new way will lead to the future of my country.

It is a letter addressed to you, because you have an important role in what's going on.

In fact, it is difficult and strange in the same time, to put in a few lines all thoughts, experiences and emotions of some years, which together made ideas to be born.

I feel as if I have to tell a story of a life time, but because I don't want to take too much of your time, I'll try to present to you only a few details.

I'm from an intellectual family, myself with the highest medical education, born and raised in a very beautiful and natural rich country, ROMANIA, which was, unfortunately, condemned and destroyed during the last 45 years by a draconic and inhuman regime.

We witnessed how our intellectuals were marginalised and how the system tried hard to destroy all the values of a country, starting with human dignity and ending with mother nature.

The only freedom we had, it was the possibility to travel in our imagination.

Maybe it's hard for you to believe and imagine a group of teenagers and later students, looking in a small room at a map, and traveling around the world. Around the free world! And each of us, telling to the others everything we knew from the books, about those places.

You also cannot imagine that the same group of friends was queuing up for hours in front of a Cinema in order to get tickets for a western movie. Sometimes 4-5 times for the same movie. It was not because of the story or because some famous actors. It was just for the fact, that it was our only possibility to get in touch with the outside world. It was just to have the possibility to see the Statue of Liberty, "peaces" of Paris, London, or New York.

2

It was just to have an idea what people have in their houses, how do they live, how do they look.

Information about recycling, green peace, protection of the nature, sounded to us like words from another planet.

Our right to freedom was heavily paid in December '89. From our group of friends, some will never see the Statue of Liberty in reality!

The last seven years brought enormous changes to my country. Things have been moving fast to "normal life" we didn't know or missed for so many years.

From economical point of view, the country is down. Reforms are taking place, for which the population is still paying hard: unemployment, poverty, not enough medical care, etc.

Everywhere now, in every town, we can hear about programs for children. Orphan children, HIV positive children, handicapped children, etc. A lot of local and international organisations are involved in helping them.

In fact, in this moment, the most neglected layer of the society is related to the old generation They've been working all their lives as slaves, they lost their lands, properties, houses, without any kind of rights and far away to be decently rewarded for their work. Now they are old, they cannot adapt to the new situation, they cannot start from the beginning, they don't understand what is happening to them. Their income is the lowest, because pensions are paid from the budget, and the budget doesn't have enough. For a country in transition, the old people are not regarded as a priority, which is sad.

The new Government of Romania brought up a lot of programs for cleaning up the country. Every Town Hall in every district, town or village is developing local programs. Unfortunately the means are low budget, and if we consider the size of Romania and the 23 million inhabitants, the action will never end. RECYCLING is a word I didn't hear so far, and what we definitely don't have in the country, is INFORMATION.

My husband is Dutch, and he was during my weak moments the only help I could rely on. He constantly told me, showed me and explained to me what Recycling means and how important it is for any country. Holland is my second home, and I am

extremely lucky to be a part of this small paradise.
I am the lucky one having the possibility to learn
about this.

I'll never forget René, (my husband) when once,
in 1992, in Bucharest, he asked me where is the col-
lecting container for empty batteries! What impressed
me was the fact, that when he discovered that these
containers don't exist in Romania, he took the empty
batteries in his pocket back to Holland and put them
there in such a container.

Then and now, I realize that what we do miss in
Romania in this field, is the simple and basic information about it! The Government can develop thou-
sands of programs, but as long as the very simple
citizen doesn't know what it is about, nothing
will happen! And as long as countries as Romania will
not do the effort to implement this to their own
population, the very educated nations concerning the
protection of the environment will not succeed in
their task, for the simple fact that the wind blows
also from our countries, and the chemicals just
thrown in the rivers or seas will poison the rest.

In fact, my idea was born in Hawaii.

The place where you helped me to think over and
over about this subject. That place which is so
incredibly beautiful, because people are concerned
about the nature. How to protect it; how to preserve
it so that the children of our children will enjoy
it as much as we did in those days.

I learned from you that the change has to come
from me and with me. I learned from you that "the
power of one" is not a sentence empty of essence!

We know very well that helping old people and
getting involved in environmental protection
projects means spending money! We have to generate
funds for this!

How to generate funds in a country with a sick
economy? How to raise funds from poor people for poor
people? How can we help ourselves?
What can we still offer as a nation in this moment?
How can we cover our wounds when they are still
bleeding?

And, after thinking and thinking, and discussing
with a lot of friends, I found the answer: ART! Wars,
Revolutions, natural calamities and draconic systems
could not destroy the spirit of my country! Our
culture, language and identity resisted over

centuries, regenerated from it's own ashes like the Phoenix bird!

All the pain, sorrows, joy, wealth and poverty, traditions and dreams, were reflected in our culture, in all her forms.

I had tears in my eyes seeing in the biggest Museums of New York, as Metropolitan, Guggenheim and Modern Art, what an important place is given to CONSTANTIN BRANCUSI Also a Romanian.

This is what we want to do: to sell art from Romania abroad. To organise exhibitions and auctions and to raise funds.

In this way, we can promote the Romanian contemporary art, and with the funds we raise, we'll help our old people to end their life with dignity.

With the funds we'll raise, we'll organise a complete mass media program about environment protection and recycling, to bring to our people the basic information and education in this field.

This is THE FIRST STEP.

Somebody has to start doing it, and I learned from you what does it mean to be "on the top of the pole."

This is another "pole" for me, my friends and my country.

Dear RAY, CHARLIE AND JOHN,

THANKS for inviting me to Hawaii, and
THANKS in advance for your support!

Dr. Ofelia Kamp
Sales Manager Romania
INTERFACE EUROPE BV
INTERFACE FLOORING BV

We closed our meeting on April 10 with an outdoor concert performed by Kenny Loggins and his band, and the Maui Symphony Orchestra. For over two years, I had envisioned that closing night. I decided that we should all be dressed in white. As all 1,100 of us stepped off the buses and walked down the hill toward an area where Kenny Loggins was to perform, I was spellbound by the scene. Our *one world learning* facilitators had our group of 1,100 form our corporate icon by filling in the chalk line that they had prepared in perfect proportion. Ray and I moved to the center of the icon as people assembled. We hired a helicopter to fly overhead and our friends from Light and Power Production Company photographed us. I looked at Ray and then I looked up and asked, "Is this hooked-up?" He said, "It looks hooked-up to me," and we gave each other a great big hug that I will never forget.

Kenny and his band conducted a magnificent concert (which included one of my favorite songs, "Celebrate Me Home"). As the evening drew to a close, we decided to do something really special. We asked everyone to lie on their backs and look at the stars, as it was a gorgeous night. We turned out all of the lights and had the Maui Symphony Orchestra play "Claire de Lune" for our closing song. It was one of those *moments in time* that I suspect no one will ever forget. I personally felt a real sense of peace and a wonderful sense of accomplishment, knowing that our meeting went exactly as I had envisioned it would.

"Claire de Lune" was Chip DeGrace's father's favorite song. Chip was chairman of our meeting, and he lost his father earlier that year.

Thanks Chip for your leadership and to you, Colleen Isom, project coordinator, for the most meaningful meeting ever conducted in the world, by a company that is truly *hooked-up*.

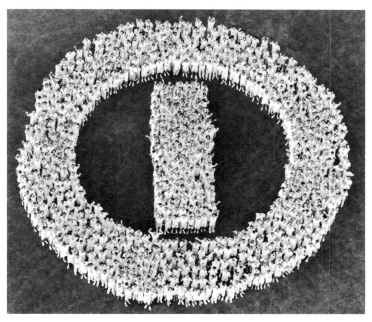

More than 1000 Interface Associates form the corporate logo during the world meeting, *One World, One Family, A Celebration,* Maui Hawaii, April 1997

STAYING THE COURSE

XI

*If you have the right formula,
all it takes is enough time and effort
for the plan to work.*

IN MARCH 1995, I published my first book, *Eitel Time: Turnaround Secrets*. At that time, our company was far from turned around, but then again, I guess there is no such thing as ever getting a company exactly where you want it. When I was writing *Eitel Time*, I remember being concerned that I was saying some things that our competitors might pick up on that they would use to their benefit. Much like in this book, I got pretty specific about some of the strategies we have employed, and if our competitors had implemented them, they would most assuredly be producing better results. It appears that they either did not read my book or may have thought I was full of *bull.*

In view of the fact that the market value of our company has moved up five-fold in the last four years, it would appear that we are implementing a pretty good plan.

You have in your hands another set of guidelines that I believe can help you improve your personal and professional life, which I hope will be of benefit to you. My guess is that none of our competitors will take any of my suggestions and ideas and put them into action. For years I have kept a quote to myself that surely will sound arrogant, but I must share it with you. It goes like this, "I will tell you every play I am going to run against you, and you still can't beat me."[16] Sometimes I will even tell you what play I'm going to run and when I'm going to run it. Here's why I know this to be true. If you figure out what you want to be and stay focused on what you want to accomplish (realizing you cannot be all things to all people), you are well on your way to achieving the goals you set.

Our competitors don't have our people, our machines, our processes, our culture, our reputation, our service, our quality, or any of the characteristics that make us special and different, and we don't have theirs.

We lead; we don't follow. Many of our competitors try to follow us but they simply don't understand that by choosing this path, they must have all the pieces of our plan to get it right the first time, or they end up with severe off-quality and waste. To put it more simply, when you try to follow a competitor, you must duplicate almost every facet of what makes you want to follow them in the first place, or you are likely to fail. Remember *same* and *similar* are different.

In March 1995, one of our competitors in LaGrange,

[16] Unknown

Georgia had the terrible misfortune of having their carpet tile plant burn to the ground. They did an excellent job of evacuating the facility, and fortunately no one was hurt. Between our two companies, we are the two major employers in town. We immediately called the president of this company and offered to help them in any way we could, including offering to manufacture products for them with our then excess capacity. They declined and instead accepted a similar offer from one of our mutual competitors, 100 miles north.

Their rivalry with us, and perhaps some jealousy of our success, was more than they could handle, so they exacerbated their problems by electing to ship material 100 miles up the road. I suppose they enjoyed thumbing their noses at us. Later that year, one of our major shareholders asked Gordon Whitener, President and CEO of Interface Americas, if he was worried about this same competitor being in a position to build a brand new plant, with the latest *state-of-the-art* equipment. Gordon's answer was right on when he said, "Yes, I am concerned; however, what I am counting on is that the same people are still running it!"

Approximately 18 months later, we learned that our company had apparently been a target of a pre-planned, corporate espionage scheme at the hands of this same competitor. The case brought by a third party against this competitor is yet to go to court.

I know of no long term benefits in following

competition. What I do know is that it is important to stay the course.

In March 1994, we purchased a business in Cartersville, Georgia, Prince Street Technologies Ltd. We thought we bought a powerful company, but when we peeled back the layers of the onion it turned out to be little more than a brand with a mediocre reputation. Rather than employing a systems approach to manufacturing, this company looked like Noah's Ark in that they had two of everything. We ended up having to implement a massive re-engineering plan, which included replacing obsolete equipment and building a new, *state-of-the-art* manufacturing facility. Approximately one year after purchasing this business, we named Joyce LaValle President and CEO. She became the highest ranking woman in our industry. Joyce asked me to mentor her along the way, which I did and continue to do. I'll never forget Joyce asking me a year or so into her role as president, "What am I doing wrong? Where are the results that you said would come?" I gave her a three word answer, "Stay the course," and she did. Today, Prince Street is setting one new record after another. Great work, Joyce!

When leaders inherit problems, which they often do, the best approach is not to blame others or make excuses, but rather to simply roll up your sleeves and get to work on the basics, and stay the course. If you have the right formula, all it takes is enough time for the plan to work. The key is to be sure you work on the basics — the blocking and tackling — every day, which reminds me of one of the greatest coaches who ever lived. Great coaches know that their players must be in shape and well-schooled in the fundamentals. Vince Lombardi always started the first practice every season with his famous line, "Gentlemen, this is a football."

In *Eitel Time*, I touched on the turnaround of Collins & Aikman Floorcoverings, a business I ran for six years, from July 1987 until November 1993. When I joined C&A, the sales of this dysfunctional division were $80 million, and they were losing approximately $2 million per month. I accepted the job after Wickes (who was then the owner), had fired the top management team for serious irregularities. There's no reason to give you all the gory details, but I can assure you it was a mess. From the very beginning, I gave it all I had, and our efforts over the following six-year period resulted in one of the better known turnaround stories in our industry.

We had a plan and we were executing it; however, when your reputation is tarnished, a turnaround simply takes longer. By the fall of 1989, I was about to meet my fifth boss. The first four were either fired or demoted. I told my newest superior that by early 1990, we would become profitable. The new co-owners in New York, venture capitalists Wasserstein Perella and Blackstone, did not believe me, so they decided to try to market the business. Their firm asking price was $55 million. I was able to raise

$42 million, and as it turned out, my offer was the only one they got, but they declined to accept it. Sure enough, we made our first profit in February 1990 ($62 thousand). Not much, but we were in the black. When I left the company three and one-half years later, we were earning $2 million per month, or 20% operating income. Last year, they sold the business for $197 million. We stayed the course during the turnaround of C&A, even though I almost got fired so many times I lost count. I also almost quit several times; however, I knew I had to stay the course until the job was done.

By late 1993, there really wasn't much for me to do because the parent company was *playing not to lose* instead of *playing to win,* and was not prepared to let the company grow. I decided to leave C&A to join Interface, and this was the best decision of my career.

Staying the course can sometimes be very tough because it is easy to get caught up in a smoke screen where we tend to make things up, based on: 1) fear; 2) guilt; and 3) an often lingering sense of one's own unworthiness. My friend, Larry Wilson, coined a great acronym utilizing *FEAR,* "*F*alse *E*vents *A*ppearing *R*eal." When we get ourselves into situations like I did at C&A, it is so easy to start making up fears that seldom have anything to do with reality. We also often end up with guilt, sometimes feeling helpless to move things fast enough. It took 32 months to turn our first profit at C&A, but we never let the criticism of our New York owners cause us to lose our self confidence. Believe me, they cared about little else except their investment. We took ownership of the problems we were dealt, but without accepting the guilt they tried to pile on us, instead choosing to stay the course and deliver the results.

The only way you can prove that you are good at something is to have the results to show for your efforts. I often laugh when I hear doctors and dentists refer to their professions as medical or dental practices. In our business lives, we are doing the same thing — practicing our best knowledge and efforts. It's kind of like raising children; by the time we figure out how to do it, they are usually grown.

Elsewhere in this book, and in previous publications, I have written of my friendship with Dr. J. Zink. A few years ago, he told me a story about a speaker he heard at a Young Presidents' Organization meeting. The speaker said a YPOer's worst nightmare is that someone will show up in his or her office one morning and matter of factly state, "It has been discovered that you don't know what you're doing." The fact is that we all learn our jobs through practice and usually have a lingering sense of unworthiness that haunts us from time to time as we prove ourselves, based on the actual results we have delivered.

Years ago, I decided that I wanted to try to be good at as many things as I could, but I knew that I must be superior in at least one thing, in order to reach the many goals I set for myself at a young age.

As it turns out, my core competency is to: 1) take complicated problems and simplify them in such a fashion that my teammates can focus on the central issues, and at the same time, 2) convince people to undertake the journey of making things right. This may be referred to as turning around businesses, but it's really about being able to see that place in the future that I talked about in Chapter One. It's also about being able to place yourself in the future and convince others to come along for the ride, and stay the course until the next challenge comes along, and then do it all over again.

NEVER LOOKING BACK

XII

*The heart of the opportunity
is inside the chest of
every one of our associates.*

IN THE LAST couple of years, I have had the pleasure of getting to know Terry Waite. Our friendship developed as a result of our company inviting him to be the opening, keynote speaker for our world meeting in Hawaii.

Prior to inviting Terry, I decided to read his book, *Taken on Trust*. In the summer of 1996, I spent part of a short vacation soaking up every word of this wonderful book. I genuinely wanted to understand why someone like Terry would attempt such a heroic feat to liberate the hostages in Lebanon. I also wanted to get to know the man. I have always been intrigued by people who believe they are being called to a mission and fearlessly take risks. Also, I always have been afraid of any thoughts of incarceration, so my curiosity was piqued.

In October 1996, I had my first opportunity to meet Terry in conjunction with an *open house* we held at our Pan European headquarters in Berkhamsted, England. I had sent him a copy of my first book, which I wasn't sure he would take the time to read. As it turned out, we sent a chauffeur driven car to pick Terry up at his home near London. We were expecting him at Berkhamsted for lunch that crisp, fall day, but before we knew it we realized it was almost 1:00 p.m., and still no Terry. Shortly thereafter, we learned that the car we had provided for him had broken down on the motor way. As you might expect, all of us were quite distressed and embarrassed. When he finally arrived at about 1:45, he stepped out of the car with a big smile on his face. I said, "Mr. Waite, I am so sorry for this problem." He said, "Not to worry, Charlie," as he held up my book, "I had plenty of *idle time* to read your book, *Eitel Time*." I immediately said, "Well, at least you know you were *Taken on Trust*." We both had a big laugh as we walked inside for a late lunch and a wonderful afternoon with our team.

We had a second meeting the following February before he actually spoke at our world meeting in April. During the course of these two get-togethers, and at our world meeting, I feel like I really got to know Terry Waite. Terry is one of the most sincere, charismatic and brave individuals I have ever known. During one of our conversations, the subject of Oliver North came up. I expected that the discussion would raise the hair on the back of Terry's neck. Without getting into too much detail, I must say that I was shocked when I realized that Terry seemed to place no blame nor harbor any anger toward Colonel North, whom many believe was responsible for Terry's capture in Lebanon. Terry made his feelings clear to me when he said, "I did what I had to do and Colonel Oliver North apparently did what he believed he had to do."

Terry was clearly at peace with himself for his brave actions and he has never looked back with any apparent regret.

The theme of our 1997 annual report is, "Why do we jump off poles?" The answer is found inside the front cover, "To discover what is possible." When Terry was attempting to liberate the hostages, he was trying to discover what was possible.

Interface is a learning company where our associates are encouraged to take risks. By the end of 1998, all of our 7,500 associates will have spent three days in a *Play to Win®* session. By asking all of our people to participate in a *one world learning* program, we help them model risk taking, which always results in personal change and growth.

As I stated earlier, we are equally as interested in sharing our learning, and for this reason, we are now helping other companies with their own challenges. We are going forward and never looking back.

To be effective, we know that we must get to the *heart of the problem* and know that heart is always in the people. Our mission is clearly to help people discover their personal vision, mission and then set goals. We don't try to tell people what they should be, but rather help them see what they can be.

Almost every enterprise has various initiatives or programs underway within its organization. When we get involved with a company, the first question we ask is, "What do you have going on in your company in the area of employee development?" Invariably, our clients end up rattling off a list of several programs, such as: 1) quality circles; 2) one or two day retreats for various levels of the organization; 3) involvement with training organizations, usually run by a current or former professor, and the list goes on. In most cases, all of these activities are worthwhile, but there is seldom a mechanism to connect them in a fashion that makes sense and lends cohesion to the entire organization.

Our role at *one world learning* is to help our clients encircle all of the programs that are in progress within their company. We can then help them connect these initiatives in a manner focused on what is most important to them. The *heart* of the opportunity is always inside the chest of their associates. We initiate this discovery process with the leadership team. As I said earlier, we require that the CEO *buy in* and participate in all efforts and activities. At *one world learning,* we don't employ sales people selling our service, but rather rely on our reputation for delivering results. We help people make the connection with their story, and use it as a source of strength. We also help individuals *let go* of old baggage and encourage them to *never look back*.

The more we have to look forward to in life, the more we realize what we have to live for. You may have noticed how most people who know they are nearing the end of their life mainly talk about the past. I said, *most,* but not all. What about George Burns who so perfectly connected with his story and used it to make so many people happy during his 100 years on this planet?

Many people believe that the last words out of his mouth were, "Gracie, here I come."

The best way to be sure you have a lot to look forward to in your life is to work to create a future that you want to live in. You can then recognize that the highest reward for your toil is not what you get for it, but what you become as a result of it. Call it "Mapping Your Legacy," if you like. If you are reading this, it is not too late! You can even start right now.

Thank you for taking time to read my book. If you have any reactions, feedback or questions please feel free to contact me at Interface, Inc., 2859 Paces Ferry Road, Suite 2000, Atlanta, Georgia 30339.

CHARLIE EITEL'S RECOMMENDED BOOKS

Mid-Course Correction Toward a Sustainable Enterprise:
The Interface Model
    AUTHOR: Ray C. Anderson
    PAPERBACK: The Peregrinzilla Press ISBN 0-9645953-5-4

Managing by Storying Around
    AUTHOR: David Armstrong
    HARDBACK: Doubleday Currency ISBN 0-385-42154-0

The One Minute Manager
    AUTHOR: Dr. Kenneth H. Blanchard and
    Dr. Spencer Johnson
    HARDBACK: William Morrow & Company, Inc.
    ISBN 0688014291
    PAPERBACK: Berkley Publishers ISBN 0425098478

The One Minute Manager Builds High Performing Teams
    AUTHOR: Dr. Kenneth H. Blanchard, Dr. Donald Carew,
    and Eunice Parisi-Carew
    HARDBACK: William Morrow & Company, Inc.
    ISBN 0-688-10972-1

The Power of Ethical Management: Why the Ethical Way is
the Profitable Way in Your Life and in Your Business
    AUTHOR: Dr. Kenneth H. Blanchard and
    Dr. Norman Vincent Peale
    HARDBACK William Morrow & Company, Inc.
    ISBN 0-688-07062-0
    PAPERBACK: Fawcett Book Group ISBN 0-449-91975-7

Journey to Center: Lessons in Unifying Body, Mind & Spirit
    AUTHOR: Thomas F. Crum
    PAPERBACK: Simon & Schuster ISBN 0-684-83922-9

The Magic of Conflict
    AUTHOR: Thomas F. Crum
    PAPERBACK: Simon & Schuster ISBN 0-684-85448-1

The Living Company
AUTHOR: Arie De Geus
HARDBACK: Harvard Business School Press
ISBN 0-87584-782X

Eitel Time: Turnaround Secrets
AUTHOR: Charlie Eitel
HARDBACK: The Peregrinzilla Press ISBN 0-9645953-0-3
PAPERBACK: Harcourt Brace & Company
ISBN 0-15-503621-1

Mapping Your Legacy, A Hook-It-Up Journey
AUTHOR: Charlie Eitel
HARDBACK: The Peregrinzilla Press ISBN 0-9645953-3-8
PAPERBACK: The Peregrinzilla Press ISBN 0-9645953-4-6

The Ecology of Commerce
AUTHOR: Paul Hawken
PAPERBACK: Harper Collins Publishers ISBN 0-88730-704-3

Growing a Business
AUTHOR: Paul Hawken
PAPERBACK: Simon & Schuster, Inc. ISBN 0-67167-164-2

The Corporate Mystic: A Guidebook for Visionaries with Their Feet on the Ground
AUTHORS: Gay Hendricks & Kate Ludeman
PAPERBACK: Bantam Books, Inc. ISBN 0-553-37494-X

Life is a Contact Sport: Ten Great Strategies That Work
AUTHORS: Ken Kragen and Jefferson Graham
HARDBACK: William Morrow & Company, Inc.
ISBN 0-688-13282-0

Ishmael
AUTHOR: Daniel Quinn
PAPERBACK: Bantam Books, Inc. ISBN 0-553-37540-7

The Fifth Discipline: The Art & Practice of the Learning Organization
    AUTHOR: Dr. Peter M. Senge
    PAPERBACK: Doubleday & Company, Inc.
    ISBN 0-385-26095-4

How to Sell at Prices Higher Than Your Competitors: The Complete Book on How to Make Prices Stick
    AUTHORS: Lawrence L. Steinmetz, Bill Brooks, Roger Dawson, and Jim Cathcart
    PAPERBACK: Horizon Publications, Inc. ISBN 0-963-19230-2

Nice Guys Finish Last: Management Myths and Reality
    AUTHOR: Lawrence L. Steinmetz
    HARDBACK: Devin-adair Publications, Inc.
    ISBN 0-815-96316-5

The Discipline of Market Leaders: Choose Your Customers, Narrow Your Focus, Dominate Your Market
    AUTHORS: Dr. Michael Treacy & Dr. Fred Wiersema
    PAPERBACK: Addison Wesley ISBN 0-201-40719-1

Taken on Trust: An Autobiography
    AUTHOR: Dr. Terry Waite
    PAPERBACK: William Morrow & Company, Inc.
    ISBN 0-688-14384-9

A Simpler Way
    AUTHORS: Margaret J. Wheatley and Myron Kellner-Rogers
    HARDBACK: Berrett-Koehler Publishers ISBN 1-881-05295-8

Changing the Game: The New Way to Sell
    AUTHORS: Larry Wilson & Hersch Wilson
    Simon & Schuster, Inc. ISBN 0-671-67135-9

Stop Selling - Start Partnering
    AUTHORS: Larry Wilson & Hersch Wilson
    PAPERBACK: John Wiley & Sons, Inc. ISBN 0-471-14741-9

Lean Thinking: Banish Waste and Create Wealth in Your Corporation
AUTHORS: James P. Womack & Daniel T. Jones
HARDBACK: Simon & Schuster ISBN 0-684-81035-2

Building Positive Self-Concept in Kids
AUTHOR: Dr. J. Zink
PAPERBACK: J. Zink Incorporated ISBN 0-942-49001-0

Dearly Beloved: Secrets of Successful Marriage
AUTHOR: Dr. J. Zink & Kern Walsh Zink
PAPERBACK: J. Zink Incorporated ISBN 0-942-49017-7

Ego States
AUTHOR: Dr. J. Zink
PAPERBACK: J. Zink Incorporated ISBN 0-942-49005-3

Face It: A Spiritual Journey of Leadership
AUTHORS: Dr. J. Zink, Ray Anderson and Charlie Eitel
PAPERBACK: The Peregrinzilla Press ISBN 0-964-59531-1

Motivating Kids
AUTHOR: Dr. J. ZInk
PAPERBACK: J. Zink Incorporated ISBN 0-942-49002-9

The Parent Your Parents Were Not
AUTHORS: Dr. J. Zink & Kern Walsh Zink
PAPERBACK: J. Zink Incorporated ISBN 0-942-49017-7

Upbringing: Raising Emotionally Intelligent Children
AUTHOR: Dr. J. Zink
PAPERBACK: The Peregrinzilla Press ISBN 0-964-59532-X

Hammer-Proof, A Positive Guide to Values-Based Leadership
AUTHOR: Dr. Jeffrey Zink Peak Press ISBN 1-892-36000-4

For anyone, whether in the world of business or the arena of personal growth, Mapping Your Legacy, A Hook-It-Up Journey *is an inspiring book, packed with the actual stories of a success story as it happened. Charlie Eitel is a good role model for anyone. He has a thinking heart, a learning mind, and a value system of highest integrity. His most outstanding quality is his unbelievably consistent, positive approach to problem solving. He does not impose limits, nor does he waste energy criticizing others. He assesses the situation, gets the vision, and proceeds to map the design with a personal magnetism that is impossible to resist. Dyed in the wool pessimists should not read this book, for they risk being converted to the other side — pure, unadulterated, and yet realistic optimism!*

Marjorie R. Barlow, L.P.C., Ph.D.

Great follow up to Eitel Time. Mapping Your Legacy, A Hook-It-Up Journey *offers great 'real world tips' on how to turn visions into reality. Charlie Eitel's narrative style as well as the personal and business perspectives that he has drawn from his own experiences add to the value of his insights.*

William M. Cameron, Chairman of the Board & Chief Executive Officer
American Fidelity Corporation

Charlie's holistic approach to the restructuring of the American company should be read by every C.E.O. and manager in the country. Employer-employee relations become human relations and companies become communities. At the core of his very human eco-sense is the development rather than the waste of human potential, which is after all the most valuable asset any company can have."

Bernadette Cozart, Founder of the Greening of Harlem Coalition
1996 Recipient (First Award) of Global Green USA's Millennium Award
for Individual Environmentalism Activism

Charlie Eitel knows how to turn a life of work into a work of art and to add great value in the process.

Tom Crum, Cofounder and President of Aiki Works and
author of *The Magic of Conflict and Journey to Center*

A rare book describing the secrets of corporate success within a personal pilgrimage towards finding one's own purpose. Eitel does not fear sharing his personal story for he knows it cannot be duplicated, only admired by students of business. He motivates us all in the way he applies the concepts of business to every aspect of his life with what appears to be ease and dedication. He is a master at making right things happen."

B. Curtis Hamm, Ph.D., Professor Emeritus, Oklahoma State University,
College of Business Administration

Mapping Your Legacy, A Hook-It-Up Journey *should be read by any would-be manager for the first decade of the 21st Century. It not only condenses in easily readable form the secret of growing a large and profitable business, it contains the insight and thinking of an executive who made it all happen."*

Lawrence L. Steinmetz, President, High Yield Management, Inc. and author of
How to Sell at Prices Higher Than Your Competitors and *Nice Guys Finish Last*